AMERICA BY THE THROAT

AMERICA BY THE THROAT

The Stranglehold of Federal Bureaucracy

by
GEORGE ROCHE

Foreword by William F. Buckley, Jr.

Hillsdale College Press
Hillsdale, Michigan

Publisher: Hillsdale College Press
Director: Peter C. McCarty
Senior Editor: Lynne Morris
Jacket Design: Carl Smith / Merlin Inc.
Book Design: Henry Johnson
Typesetting: Littlepage Graphics, Port Chester, NY
and Colonial Press, Inc., Jackson, MI

Manufactured in the United States of America.

Library of Congress Cataloging in Publication Data

Roche, George Charles.
AMERICA BY THE THROAT

1. Bureaucracy — United States
2. Bureaucracy
I. Title JK421.R55 1985   353'.01   85-080099
ISBN 0-916308-97-9

To Carolyn,
whose loyalty and intelligence
make so many projects a success.

HILLSDALE
COLLEGE PRESS

PUBLISHER'S NOTE

Hillsdale College is marked by its strong independence and its emphasis on academic excellence. It holds that the traditional values of Western civilization, especially those fundamental to a free society of responsible individuals, are worthy of defense. In maintaining these values, the College has remained independent throughout its history, neither soliciting nor accepting government funding for its operations.

In keeping with the College's educational mission, the Hillsdale College Press offers other books by George Roche; the *Champions of Freedom* series from the Ludwig von Mises Lecture Series on economic policy; *Imprimis*, the monthly journal of the Center for Constructive Alternatives; *The Essential Imprimis* collection; *The Christian Vision* series from Hillsdale's Christian Studies Program annual convocation; the CCA-Shavano video and cassette tapes; and the easy-to-read, humorous *Alternatives* program materials to explain the economic and political facts of life.

America by the Throat is a devastating, no-holds-barred documentation of the bureaucratic nightmare, and a reasoned analysis of the means by which Americans can pull themselves out of the morass. Hillsdale President George Roche's wit is sharp and irreverent, in the manner of American protest since the Boston Tea Party. The book's scholarly roots come from Roche's association with the late economist Ludwig von Mises, and will be read along with Mises' classic *Bureaucracy*, as it examines the West's slide into bureaucratic paralysis.

Peter C. McCarty
Director

Lynne Morris
Senior Editor

CONTENTS

Foreword

Reading this book causes something one can describe without exaggeration as pain. But it is a salvific pain, because it generates a purposive indignation. You may say: Ah, but the problems of bureaucracy are always with us. Reading George Roche isn't like reading Harriet Beecher Stowe's *Uncle Tom's Cabin*. There you knew what had to be done: you needed to emancipate the slaves. But here you are face to face with the human character as it is impressed on the civil order, and there is nothing you can do.

Indeed, George Roche early in his book warns us that he has written a descriptive, not a prescriptive book. But then Mrs. Stowe in fact did not stipulate how exactly the life of the slaves was to be improved, satisfying herself to describe what their life was like. So Mr. Roche has described what government does, giving rise to bureaucracies that thrive in asphyxiative regulations. How does one contend with this?

Mr. Roche (and, indeed other critics of big government) points out that much legislation is justified as "reform" legislation: *i.e.,* measures that seek to improve on other measures that should never have been passed in the first place. For such legislation he tends to have contempt. Acknowledging the danger of yet more legislation, I think that even so, I would back a bill establishing an Office of Ombudsman, cabinet rank, with the single mandate that it collect and bring to the attention of the president for executive action all federal regulations that are sclerotic in effect, and that that agency also collect all examples of unnecessary laws that hamper social energy, for the purpose of remedial legislation.

In the past ten years, a protocol has been born on the waters near where I live. Suddenly—it happened almost overnight—the boating public, motivated by the *crise de coeur* of ecologists—decided they would stop tossing their garbage into the water. Not everyone, mind you, but a great majority, and it has made a huge difference. Suddenly, when the Office of the Ombudsman got into full swing, people would begin to identify, and then to report, those awful accretions that so dissipate human energy and will; and then, some day, peering into the forest of laws and regulations, you would open spaces and breathe air, even as, looking at Lake Erie today, one can see the beginning of true regeneration. Needless to say, I would insist that this be called the Roche Act.

William F. Buckley, Jr.

INTRODUCTION

Herbert Spencer once noted that on any given day, you could read two stories in the papers about the failures of government programs — and three stories about pleas for *new* government programs to do even more for us!

That was over a hundred years ago, in England, but the point rings truer than ever for us today. The only difference is that now we see more stories about a certain kind of failure, one that seems to us mindless and mean. Such a story might read like this: " The Occupational Safety and Health Administration (OSHA) today ordered the University of Illinois to tear down the handrails alongside walkways on campus, and to install new handrails exactly 42 inches high. According to OSHA, the old handrails are several inches too low to comply with regulations."

The story happens to be true. And when we read it, we know at once here is the federal bureaucracy at work. It may even give us a chuckle — who else but a bureaucrat would be so boneheaded as to insist that handrails must be exactly 42 inches high, and not one inch higher or lower? But it is not so funny when you learn that Illinois had to pay over $500,000 to change those handrails. If it weren't for a petty bureaucratic rule, the money could have been used, say, to hire fifteen full professors, or build a dormitory wing, or add three thousand volumes to the school library.

It is precisely this sort of perverse and hurtful waste

that increasingly marks the failure of government actions today. *The problem is bureaucracy, and bureaucracy has become a national epidemic.* The federal bureaucracy has more than *tripled* in size in the last ten years. It is *ten times* as large and powerful as it was twenty years ago, at the beginning of the Kennedy–Johnson years. It has swollen a *thousand-fold* in power in the last half century. This titanic expansion of bureaucratic power is shattering the foundations of a free society and menacing the well-being of every citizen. The federal government, designed and intended to be the Servant of the people, now bids to become our Master.

Such is the problem I address in this book, and it has already grown to proportions that are difficult to grasp. "Bureaucracy," in the abstract, is hardly a new concern. And if the problem were no more than a few harmless bumblers in dusty federal offices, we would have little to worry about. However, a bureaucratic machine so swollen and powerful that it can hold sway over every citizen is indeed a new — and ominous — development in American life. How this situation came to be, what it portends, and what we can do about it, are questions every intelligent American ought to ponder. Soon.

We are all aware that the federal government itself has grown immense in recent times. It is not as well understood, unfortunately, that as government grows, it necessarily becomes more and more bureaucratic and rigid — and authoritarian. The overweening bureaucracy that emerges is less an evil in itself than a reflection of this trend and a greater evil: the thrust toward an all-powerful central government.

For fifty years and more, the dominant opinion in or near the seats of power has worked ceaselessly to erect a federal State on the Old World model: paternalistic, autocratic, and utterly alien to the American constitutional ideal. This effort has imposed on us the largest, most costly, most bureaucratic State in all of history, where once we had and long cherished the smallest.

Every extension of federal power has brought with it new bureaucratic controls and interferences in our lives. This is unavoidable. Bureaus are the handmaidens of political power. They are required by law as well as practical necessity to act as they do, however inflexible, small-minded, and destructive their actions may seem to the rest of us. Such are, and always have been, the consequences of the authoritarian State.

It is in the nature of bureaucracy ever to work "by the book," reducing every aspect of our lives to suffocating rules and lifeless averages. Rulebook methods are the only way State power can be organized. There is no room for intelligent decisions and flexibility. The bureaucratic State, William F. Rickenbacker has written, is ". . . the very opponent and negation of human freedom and individuality. Men strive to excel, the State seeks after averages. Men covet novelty, the State extrapolates from yesterday. Men love to chaffer person to person, the State is a rule book. Men yearn to be free, the State is the sum of liberties lost."

The bureaucracy has at its disposal one tool only, and that is force: coercive power. This tool has its purposes, but is totally unsuited to the direction of economic or private matters. Most applications of this power in the private sector, unfortunately, cause more harm than good.

Certainly, much of the malaise America has suffered in recent years can be traced directly to the use of bureaucratic power where it does not belong. Our energies as a free people are thwarted by the snarl of red tape and rules. Our schools deteriorate year after year, in exact proportion to the growth of a gigantic educational bureaucracy. Business and industry, chained by literally millions of regulations, are less and less able to provide the jobs and goods we need. The poor, the aged, the disadvantaged, the hurt and handicapped, all supposedly the beneficiaries of government aid, instead become its victims, caught in an endless web of rules and frustrations. Our hopes of bettering our lives, our very dreams, falter under the burdens the bureaucracy imposes.

Half a century's experimentation with do-everything government has proven to be a monstrous, heartbreaking mistake. Instead of "solving" social problems, it has created new and far greater ones. Its ideas and programs go forward on their own momentum despite being repeatedly discredited by practical experience. Its cost is so great as to ennervate the most productive economy the world has ever seen. Its accumulated powers could emerge as totalitarianism in any severe crisis; and a crisis is sure to come if the statist trend continues. In the end, we too could face the fate that has marked every Old World State, every civilization before us: a progressive weakening of society by State exactions, leading to degeneracy, collapse, and death. No people before us who have made the same mistakes, who have chosen to put their faith in the State, have ever escaped this doom. Nor shall we.

* * *

How do we get back on the right track? How do we bring bureaucracy back under control? How do we strip the bureaucracy of its illegitimate powers and return them to the people?

I have no full or satisfying answer to these questions. This book is diagnostic, not prescriptive. It is not intended to be a blueprint for the changes needed. Such a blueprint may not exist. Historical experience offers little comfort and less advice about how to escape our dilemma.

What I do know is that one election will change little,

however much it is a step in the right direction. The problem can be fought in the electoral process, but it cannot be solved there. It runs much deeper than politics; it is a problem of our hearts and minds, of our values and choices. It is a moral problem. Each of us must in his own way find and restore and burnish the values that animated the American Republic at its beginning. With the wisdom of our fathers, we must respect in full the rights of life and liberty and property, for these are the cornerstones of all civilization. But more than this we must abandon the false religion of the State, and renew our faith in the sovereignty of our Creator and His Law. Without this, we will not succeed. So it is ordained.

George Roche
Hillsdale, Michigan

I

BUREAUCRACY: ENEMY OF THE PEOPLE

"He hath erected a multitude of New Offices and sent hither swarms of officers to harass our people, and eat out their substance."
— America's complaint about King George III and British rule, in the Declaration of Independence, 1776

Thomas Jefferson never heard of "bureaucracy," but nobody has described it more movingly than he did in the Declaration of Independence. It was to be free of bureaucracy and taxes that the colonists dared fight the mighty British empire. In that great revolution, subjects of the King became free Americans. They thought they would be free forever.

In pitifully few years, Jefferson was again obligated to warn us about bureaucracy, only this time the threat was from our own government rather than the British:" . . . [w]hen we must wait for Washington to tell us when to sow and when to reap," Jefferson wrote, "we shall soon want for bread."

Alas, the warning went unheeded. In the course of time the federal government built the biggest bureaucratic machine the world has ever seen. On a scale the kings of England never dreamed of, it has erected multitudes of new offices and sent forth swarms of officers to harass our people and eat out our substance. We call them bureaucrats.

No American today is safe from federal bureaucrats. If you eat, drink, breathe air, dress, work, play, go to school, drive, read, watch TV, listen to radio, travel, own a house, rent an apartment, operate a farm, run a business, buy, sell, advertise, publish, spend money, save money, borrow money, invest, ship goods, import and export, use the mails, have children, get sick, or grow old, you are automatically in the grasp of at least one major federal bureau, and within reach of scores or hundreds more. If you think you can escape by dying, you haven't reckoned on the ultimate bureau, the Internal Revenue Service.

To the private citizen, the activities of the federal bureaucracy may be bewildering, frustrating, wasteful, costly, or at times, hilarious. But too often its effects are tragic. The bureaucracy has wrapped the hurt and the needy in a web of rules, leaving them helpless and without hope. It has destroyed families. It has used free Americans in bizarre experiments that have drugged, crippled, blinded, and killed people. It has deformed, paralyzed, and killed people with dangerous drugs, and left countless thousands to suffer or die by denying them needed medicines. Its cost to each of us, in liberty and opportunity lost, as well as dollars, is brutal. Under feudalism, the serfs only had to work three months a year for the masters. *You* have to work four to support federal bureaucrats, and another month for state and local bureaucrats.

Not a day passes but that bureaucratic actions are blasted in editorials, or held up as examples of waste, futility, and sheer dizziness. Bureaucrats are the butt of endless jokes and cartoons. No one will even admit to being one. Ask a convention of bureaucrats what they do, and not one will stand and announce with pride, "I'm a bureaucrat." Yet there are millions of them around, and they seem to proliferate like mosquitoes in a fever swamp — with about the same contribution to human happiness.

Bureaucrats' vexatious methods have actually made it into the dictionary. According to Webster's *Third New International Dictionary*, unabridged, bureaucracy is "a system in administration marked by constant striving for increased functions and power, by lack of initiative and flexibility, by indifference to human needs or public opinion, and by a tendency to defer decisions to superiors and to impede action with red tape." Not exactly Jeffersonian in eloquence, but there you have it: the Bureaucrat is power-hungry, inflexible, indifferent to human needs, servile, and draped in red tape. Disgruntled citizens could no doubt expand on this description at length.

Bureaus rule you with rules. There are often dozens and sometimes hundreds of bureaus regulating a given activity. Every one of those bureaus has thousands of rules, and some have millions. If you look closely, you'll find rules in any bureau that contradict other rules, which in turn contradict rules in other bureaus. They can get you coming and going. An activity may be officially encouraged and discouraged, legal and illegal, required and prohibited, all at the same time. And every bureaucratic rule is binding. A bureaucrat need only dream up a regulation, publish it in the *Federal Register*, and it's the law. Nobody has ever read all the rules and regulations on the books. Nobody can count them. Yet if you run afoul of a single bureaucratic rule, out of all the uncounted millions of them, you may find yourself pinned under a bureaucrat's thumb.

This is madness. People do not live their lives the bureaucratic way, "by the book," nor do they want to. It is not normal, it is not natural. Force and force alone can impose such arbitrary and unnatural rules on our lives. If the rules were *good* for us, why would force ever be needed?

The rules we follow in private life are few, simple, and moral in nature. We do not obey the Ten Commandments because somebody forces us to, at gunpoint. We obey them because doing so enriches our lives and puts us in harmony with those around us.

Indeed, much or most of what we do in life has nothing at all to do with rules. What guides us is self-interest or motivation. That is, we do things because we enjoy them, or because they improve our condition and enhance our satisfactions in life. We deal with one another freely and voluntarily, meeting our differing needs, and resolving our differences, without force, in the marketplace. We cannot, after all, force others to do our bidding; that is slavery, and it is repugnant to those of us who would be free. Yet our own normal, free-willed, self-supporting actions as responsible people are just as repugnant to the bureaucrat.

The dedicated bureaucrat believes that all of life must be brought under the control of his rules. He may acknowledge that no one rule can possibly fit millions of individuals in millions of situations. But to him, it just means that he should have millions of rules to cover everything, all of them imposed by force. Millions of rules are exactly what he has today. And force is a government monopoly.

In a word, the bureaucratic mind and methods are *fundamentally* different from, and irreconcilable with, private life, the things we do in a free and normal way. The logic of bureaucratic coercion is that we, the people, cannot do things right on our own, cannot be trusted, and must be reduced to serfdom in the bureaucratic order. This, from so-called "civil servants" who supposedly work at our pleasure and are supported by our money and labor. The Servant has become Master.

* * *

What we call "bureaucracy," then, is the imposition of arbitrary rules, by force — literally, "rule by bureau." If we may judge it by its fruits, as we judge everything else, the wonder is that it could possibly exist. The bureaucracy is every bit as insane in practice as it is in theory.

"Dizziness" is not one of the bureaucratic qualities that made it into Webster's, but it should have been. People are forever using words like bonkers and wacko to describe it. Almost everybody I talk to has a pet horror story about bureaucracy, and the craziness of it is among the most persistent themes. I have a large collection of these stories, a few of which I'll share with you. First let me note that bureaucrats themselves are not crazy — at least no more so than anybody else. Most are known to lead quite normal lives, after they get off work at night. It's what they do on the job, "by the rules," that's wacky. Anyone else would see instantly that a given action is ridiculous; not the servant of the rulebook. He sees only the rules.

This is what we call the "bureaucratic mind" and here is some of its routine handiwork:[1]

- Federal bureaucrats drew up specifications for a mousetrap. The specs ran 700 pages long and weighed 3.3 pounds.

- The famous Abominable Snowman, also known as Bigfoot, Yeti, or Sasquatch, is on the federal endangered species list, in case somebody ever discovers one.

---

[1] Many of these items are thanks to *National Review* magazine, which for years has had an impish delight in chronicling bureaucratic boneheadedness. Its pages are by now probably the best single source of such material.

• The National Endowment for the Arts financed a film that repeatedly showed a dog being shot to death.

• The National Institute for Mental Health granted a professor $97,000 to study what he called the "social and behavioral relationships" in a Peruvian brothel. (Which worked out to $177 a night for the tireless researcher. Crazy Gringos!)

• The Federal Voting Rights Act specifies that areas that have a significant minority who speak a language other than English must be given ballots in the other language. Which is why federal bureaucrats, on behalf of the Lumbee Indians, ordered three counties of North Carolina to print ballots in Lumbee. The only trouble is, there is no Lumbee language. There was once, but the Lumbees abandoned it when white settlers moved into the area. The beleaguered North Carolina officials considered applying for a federal grant to invent a new Lumbee language and teach it to the Lumbees.

• Every year the Defense Department buys 48,000 heavy duty leather holsters for .45 caliber pistols. It has not gotten any new .45 pistols since 1945.

• In a surprise economy move, the Department of Health, Education, and Welfare decided after six years and half a million dollars, that it might not continue providing $81,000 a year to teach 28 Navajo medicine men the arts of ceremonies and taboos.

• Federal bureaucrats poured 76 million barrels of oil into a cave to create a "Strategic Petroleum Reserve," only to learn that they had forgotten to install pumps to get it out again.

• After a long delay, the White House finally took decisive action on streamlining federal aid programs. It issued an 11-volume study on the subject.

• David Berkowitz, the famed "Son of Sam" killer, has been receiving Social Security payments of some $300 a month in prison because he was ruled "mentally ill" and "unable to work."

• The Food and Drug Administration issued an urgent warning to the public not to *eat* those heart-shaped boxes your Valentine candies come in.

"Wonderland" is Washington, D.C.'s middle name, thanks to bureaucracy. But bureaucracy infects every level of government and every type of government. At times it seems that the state and local bureaucrats strive to do things even zanier and weirder than their big brothers in Wonderland, D.C.

- The government of Calumet Township, Indiana, nabbed one of its employees using witchcraft to get a welfare client to take part in a food stamp fraud. To avoid a recurrence, the city banned "voodoo, witchcraft, spiritualism and spells."

- California officials ruled that Mr. Ted Giannoulas can be a chicken anywhere but in San Diego. Whereupon Mr. Giannoulas became a parrot, and considered an offer to be a chicken in Atlanta, Georgia, where it's legal. Eventually he was permitted to be a chicken even in San Diego, so long as he was a *different* chicken.

- Seattle emergency vehicles helped deliver six babies one year, five of them to women.

- When George Willig climbed the World Trade Center in New York, he was arrested for "scaling a building without a permit," fined $1.10, and forced to eat lunch with Mayor Beame. Which New York bureau sells building scaling permits was not disclosed.

- Mr. Arnold Weber of Carmel, New York, was fined $320 for keeping an unlicensed cougar. To find the cougar license bureau, go three doors past the building scaling office and turn left.

- A man in Morganton, North Carolina, was fined $52 and given a suspended jail sentence for biting the tail off a snake.

- Police on a training mission in St. Louis planted several pounds of dynamite under the bumper of a civilian car in an airport parking lot. Before the trainees, using dogs, could find it, the owners retrieved their car and drove away.

- Unable to convict its rider, Idaho authorities filed suit against a 1970 Honda 750 motorcycle, for allegedly transporting marijuana.

• A Colorado woman who wants to be cremated on a funeral pyre when she dies made the dreadful mistake of asking whether it was legal. With faultless bureaucratic logic, her request was routed to the Colorado Air Pollution Control Board. Groping for just the right rule, and with the utmost in bureaucratic delicacy, the board ruled that the lady would need a permit — under the statute that prohibits the unauthorized burning of rubbish and trash.

Needless to say, wacky doings by bureaucrats are not limited to American government. Bureaucracy exists in every country, without regard to race, creed, sex, political system, or previous condition of servitude. It may have its own national or local flavor, but you know at once it's the bureaucratic mind at work when, for instance, Belgium made it a crime to show mercy to a caterpillar. The FDA-types in Denmark banned the coloring in Coca Cola, but do permit Danes to drink gray Coke. The Soviet bureaucracy is in such desperate condition that it bought mail handling equipment from *us*, to improve its postal service. But we'll let other countries worry about their own bureaucrats. Ours are quite enough to fret about, and besides, as a patriotic American, I happen to think that American bureaucrats can outwacko, outwaste, and outboondoggle any foreign competitors.

Behind dizziness, the quality about bureaucrats that most impresses people is their enormous capacity to waste money. *Our* money. Nobody wastes money more efficiently than Washington's corps of bureaucrats. Its appetite for waste is legendary, its skill at squandering is internationally renowned, and its budget will soon be measured in light-years. Federal bureaucrats not only waste money here but all over the world. They've even managed to waste some on the moon, on Venus, on Mars, Jupiter, Saturn and points west. In one case they even managed to blast a bureaucratic boondoggle clean out of our solar system,[2] a first in history.

Now, I don't think bureaucrats *try* to waste money. They don't get up in the morning and say, "I'm going to go down to the office and squander a bundle today." Some, a few, even try not to. However, for reasons we'll discuss later on, it's impossible for bureaucracy *not* to waste money. The wastage is inherent, built right into the bureaucratic method. The term "bureaucratic waste" is almost redundant. Combine this inherent tendency to waste money with the astronomical sums in the hands of federal bureaucrats, and you get stories like these. As the saying goes, easy come, easy go:

- The Federal Aviation Administration spent $57,800 studying stewardesses and determined that their noses average 2.18 inches long.

- The Pentagon spends $13.53 to make a grilled cheese sandwich.

- In 1978, U.S. Public Health hospitals were spending $6 million a year for plastic surgery — mainly facelifts for the wives of top military brass.

- The new Department of Energy, trying desperately to justify its existence, announced the discovery of a vast new source of energy, with reserves equal to 250 billion barrels of oil: peat. Ten billion dollars a year for these boneheads, and they tell us to burn swamps.

- According to a National Science Foundation study costing $918,000, people who go camping do not like bugs or mosquitoes.

---

[2] I refer to the Voyager spacecraft. I'm not criticizing its main, scientific mission, which included sending back those breathtaking photos of Saturn. The bureaucrats got into the act by putting a phonograph aboard, with a recorded message of greetings from Earth, in numerous languages. Just in case some Higher Intelligence out there finds the thing some day, see. And figures out how to work the phonograph. And happens to speak English, or Mandarin Chinese, or Tagalog, or Quechua. Fittingly enough, the record is made of solid gold. If there is any Higher Intelligence out there, it won't have any trouble figuring out that this was the bureaucratic mind at work.

• In 1977, to save money, the Department of Energy decided to move to more austere quarters. Secretary Schlesinger had to give up his private dining room and Deputy Secretary O'Leary lost his shower. The move cost $17 million.

• Federal bureaucrats spend some $8 billion a year on travel, an average of $3,000 apiece.

• The Environmental Protection Agency has a lengthy application form with a $10 fee for farmers to discharge waste water on their own property. It costs the EPA $15.09 to process a farmer's check, and $376.10 to process an application.

• When a leak developed in the roof of the Kennedy Center in Washington, the bureaucrats spent $4,700,000 to fix it.

• As long as we're going through the roof, we may as well note that a $65,000 emergency repair to the ceiling of the National War College was finally completed for only $1,900,000.

• "No less an authority than *The New York Times* confirms the frightening fact that: 'Washington Unable to Spend Funds as Rapidly as It Planned This Year.' It also confirms that the experts are in pothers and dithers at this unexplained federal lethargy that leaves some eight billion dollars unslushed. Holy Keynes! That's a whole week's worth of slops untroughed, influence unpeddled, voters unbought and doggles unbooned. If the professionals can't waste it fast enough, what will become of us all?"

— *National Review* item, 1976

There is another, subtler sort of waste that results when bureaucrats, as they love to do, undertake projects of monumental triviality. This reflects a fact that people outside of government can scarcely grasp: true bureaucrats have no specific, definable job. For all their endless rules, there are no true guidelines as to what they are supposed to do or how well they are doing it. It is precisely this lack of guidelines, this institutional aimlessness, that sets bureaucracy apart from productive human activity. It is, in fact, what forces bureaucrats to operate "by the rules" instead of by their productivity or profit. We will encounter this factor over and over. Its effect is to make bureaucrats search constantly for actions on the job that *look* good, look important, look normal. Yet the same lack of guidelines blinds them to what really is good, normal, important, productive. Thus we often find bureaucrats pouring their energy — not to mention our money — into enterprises that are simply ludicrous. And, indeed, examples of these exercises in triviality can sound awfully funny. Inwardly, though, I am more inclined to sorrow at things so wasteful of human endeavor.

In any case, here are a few examples of how farfetched bureaucratic projects can become:

> • "The Consumer Products Safety Commission, established October 27, 1972 for the purpose of reducing unreasonable risk of injury associated with consumer products — estimated 1976 fiscal year budget for policy development and support, $1,780,000; hazard identification, $3,950,000; hazard analysis and remedy, $10,233,00; information and education, $3,883,000; compliance and enforcement, $11,264,000; administration, $5,388,000; administrative law judges, $97,000; 890 full-time and 45 equivalent full-time positions, average paid employment 910, average salary, $17,916, total personnel compensation $18,427,000 plus $1,658,000 in benefits, total budget $36,595,000 — has ordered the manufacturer to recall an unspecified quantity of Blobo Plastic Bubb-A-Loons."
>
> — *National Review*, 1976

> • In its never-ending effort to protect American health, the FDA sued the manufacturers to force the recall of the Relco Bark Trainer and Wuf-E-Nuf electric dog collars.

> • In June, 1973 the FDA, which thrives on triviality, ruled that all cherry pies sold in interstate commerce had to contain at least 24% cherries by weight, and no more than 15% blemished cherries, opening any number of jobs for cherry inspectors to snatch away the sixteenth blemished cherry out of every hundred that passed down the line. In the same

month it announced that its next public health concern would be feminine hygiene sprays. A month later, after blasting breakfast cereals for lack of nutritional value, it blasted cereal makers for putting *more* vitamins and minerals into cereals. In December, 1975, it averted a tragedy of staggering proportions by forcing the recall of 17,000 cases of possibly dangerous pimentoes, forestalling a recall of untold millions of martinis. In November, 1976, it took decisive action to recall 500 cases of strawberry jam and 80,000 orange suckers, while assuring the public that the items were perfectly harmless.

This cascade of triviality from a single agency should give you a sharp picture of bureaucracy in general. Now consider that the FDA has perhaps the single most important assignment of any bureau, protecting our health — a life-or-death question to over 200 million Americans — and it worries about electric dog collars. Surely that will give you the idea. Yet I haven't even mentioned my very favorite story about the FDA, which goes back to October 1973. At that time, on an emergency basis, the FDA forced makers to recall glue in aerosol cans, a product almost indispensable to graphic artists for layout work. Why? Because it said it had discovered, God knows how, that spray glue would cause birth defects if *eaten* by pregnant women. Well, you know how it is with pregnant women. And bureaucrats.

"Studying" things sounds productive and important, so it has become perhaps the most popular of all bureaucratic ventures in triviality.

• Study of cultural, economic, and social impact of rural road construction in Poland — $85,000. Chasing wild boars in Pakistan — $35,000. Environmental testing of a zero gravity toilet (and I'd rather not think about what such tests entail) — $230,000. Analysis of violin varnish — $5,000. Study to find out why people say "ain't" — $121,000. Study to find out why kiddies fall off tricycles — $19,300. Study of frisbees — $375,000.

All of these, you ought to know, are from a single year, 1974, and don't even scratch the surface.

If the bureaucrats have any favorite thing to study, it's sex. Frankly, I didn't expect this at all. I would have thought bureaucracy would be as sexless as white bread. But it turns out that they are obsessed with sex, and lavish tax dollars without number on studies of the subject. Some of this — at least, if you dwell on it as much as the bureaucrats do — may seem pretty kinky, so parental discretion is advised.

> • Study of Polish bisexual frogs —$6,000. National Science Foundation grant for studying polygamy among birds — $22,000. Study of the sexual strategies of milkweed — $24,000. Investigating the sociosexual behavior of the dabbing African black duck —$81,300. Study of whether marijuana stimulates men sexually —$121,000. (That one caused quite an uproar, because it involved giving male volunteers an illegal drug to start with, followed by showing them provocative movies, and measuring the results, and you can just imagine. And remember, you and I helped finance it.) My favorite tale of the bunch concerns the Department of Agriculture's efforts, in 1976, to peep at the screwing of sexworms, or perhaps it was the sex life of screwworms, and anyway the plan was to go out and catch a bunch of screwworm flies and tie little bitty electronic diode dinguses around their necks or something, and then watch what they do with lady screwworm flies on a sort of microwave radar, and all this for only $58,480.

No mention of the monumental trivialities of the federal bureaucracy would be quite complete without equal time for the monumental stupidities. But I'm afraid that even to touch the subject would be to open the floodgates. Besides, by citing stupidities, I would hardly be teaching you anything new about bureaucracy. Let me, then, tell you just one story as a gorgeous examplar of bureaucratic stupidity. It doesn't even involve the feds. It happened in Alabama, in 1977, to a 12-year-old boy.

• Jamie Ray, 12, of Florence, Alabama, got into big trouble with the law because his treehouse was too comfortable. Jamie's treehouse, measuring 8 x 12 feet, has a shingled roof, glass windows, and carpeting. Who shows up but the city's building inspection department (treehouse division?), to rule that the treehouse was "fit for human habitation." It then determined that Jamie's treehouse was less than 20 feet away from a city street, in violation of the zoning laws. Saying he was "admittedly sympathetic," but that "my responsibility is enforcement," the building inspector gave Jamie ten days either to destroy the treehouse or to move the tree.

We have to look at all this stupidity and waste with a smile. Taken seriously, it is just too upsetting, too sad to think about. It is human resources that are being wasted, our sustenance today, our dreams for tomorrow, and ultimately some part of our lives — wasted in astronomical numbers. The saddest part of all is that *none* of it is necessary. Almost every task given the bureaucracy to do, and do at such horrendous cost, can be handled in other, better ways. Indeed, throughout most of our history, we have handled these matters with non-bureaucratic methods, not only at far less cost, but with much greater success and justice. Surely we can do this again, once we understand the enormity of the bureaucratic failure.

We have seen the bureaucratic mind at work, and chronicled its prodigious waste. But there are many other qualities about bureaucracy that compound the distress it causes, and that we must be aware of. It is, for instance, notoriously slow in getting anything done — if it succeeds at all. It is famous for bumbling and bungling. In fact, when bureaus are created to solve social problems, they have an immediate vested interest in making those problems *worse*, to expand their own functions and power. Moreover, bureaus are rewarded not by the success of their efforts, but by their *size*. The bigger one gets, the more prestige and money it commands. The more you expand your empire, the more warm bodies you command, the higher your rank in the bureaucracy.

Its "by the rules" methods make bureaucracy notoriously unresponsive and indifferent to human need. Nobody suffers more at the hands of bureaucracy than its most needy "clients." This bureaucratic attitude leads, at times, to projects with a horrifying disregard for people's rights and even their lives.

What bureaus do care about is themselves. It is common for relief agencies to spend the large majority of their funds on themselves, and allow only a trickle of payments to those in need.

Bureaucracy is perpetually plagued with graft and fraud. This, like waste, seems inherent and ineradicable. Internal auditing and controls are so weak in bureaus that swindles are easy. Multiplying this problem enormously are the vast sums of money that pass through bureaucratic hands (sticking to many). Ultimately, of course, you and I pay for all this.

Everyone hates the endless paperwork, forms, and red tape associated with bureaucracy. The cost, in dollars and hours, is staggering, yet the bureaucrats demand more. The burden grows every year.

Other unpleasant qualities bureaucracy is known for include its inflexibility, its mindless meddling, and its authoritarianism.

As an educator, I have one other major grump about bureaucrats, namely, their capacity to expeditiously formulate, study, identify, develop, coordinate, recommend, administer, and finalize the dysfunctionization of intrasocietal linguistic modalities — which is to say, butcher the English language.

Examples of all of these bureaucratic failings find their way into the news every day. It would be profitable to ponder a few of them, if only in self defense. Know thine enemy!

The mills of bureaucracy grind slowly, but exceedingly coarse.

- The FDA banned sodium cyclamate in 1969 — 19 years after its researchers found evidence that the artificial sweetener causes tumors.[3]

- After more than three years of effort by its staff of 800, the Consumer Products Safety Commission issued its first hazardous product safety standard. The hazardous product: swimming pool slides.

In bureaucracy, "slow" can mean "never."

- Since its establishment in 1938, the Civil Aeronautics Board had not "certificated" — its own word for approval — a single new trunk airline, until the deregulation of the 1980s.

The dictionary says "bungling" is doing things badly, clumsily, or in an awkward manner; mishandling or botching things. Washington's talent for it is such that the term "bureaucratic bungling" has become a cliche.

- In an effort to help the rare and endangered Kirtland Warbler by clearing away some brush, the U.S. Forest Service set fire to the bird's nesting area and burned out 25,000 acres.

- A hospital annex in San Francisco was built for the sole purpose of being torn down and rebuilt a year later, all at federal expense, into the new hospital that was needed in the first place, but for which no federal funds were available.

- The Army Corps of Engineers built two outhouses near Hastings, Minnesota. They were four-holers, with no heat or water, engineered "to meet federal environmental guidelines," and cost $25,000 each.

---

[3]The preponderant evidence today is that cyclamates are perfectly safe used in moderation. Yet the FDA is just as steadfast in refusing to allow its sale today as it was in refusing to ban it earlier. This is of no small concern, since obesity is the nation's number one health problem, and the only other artificial sweetener, saccharin, is suspected of being harmful.

• A Securities and Exchange Commission reply to a congressional questionnaire took 13,000 pages and stood fifteen feet high.

• The IRS granted tax-exemption status to a "church" and two "charitable" organizations running homosexual boys' camps and peddling pedophilic pornography.

If that one surprises you, you don't know anything about the IRS. Or its friends.

We turn to a much more serious matter. A lot of people seem to have an endless and almost childlike faith that government agencies actually do what they are supposed to do. This is sadly mistaken, and it is the kind of public support that keeps the bureaucrats in power. If we *really* judged the bureaucracy by its results, it would be out of office tomorrow. Instead, we judge it by appearances, or take it for granted. If the government creates an "Environmental Protection Agency," it's protecting the environment — right? Wrong. Terribly wrong.

There are two rock-solid reasons that bureaus do not perform as advertised. First, they are not supposed to. Their real purpose is to serve themselves and enhance government power. Their ostensible assignment is merely a tool to this end. Second, it is not in the bureau's self-interest to do its job. If it solved the problem at hand, it would be out of work — a prospect contrary to every bureaucratic instinct. Its real interest is to make the problem worse, so that it can increase its own power and authority. The EPA, for example, only occasionally prohibits practices that rape the environment; usually, it *licenses* them. Fees payable to itself, of course.

In case you have any doubts at all about these points, let me give you three examples of how government really operates when it says it is protecting the environment. The first is a classic case of an agency creating the problem it is supposed to solve.

• On January 1, 1975, the U.S. Steel Company shut down its pollution-belching open hearth furnaces in Gary, Indiana. What federal agency frantically urged U.S. Steel to fire up the furnaces and start polluting again? The Environmental Protection Agency, of course. It seems the EPA had taken U.S. Steel to court and got a ruling that fined the company $2,300 a day — $2,000 payable to itself, the other $300 to the city of Gary — for each day the company continued polluting. So the company shut down, saying its operation either "is environmentally acceptable, or it is not — and doesn't become acceptable with the payment of a daily fine." With $2,000 a day at stake, the EPA practically begged U.S. Steel to pollute. Russell Train, head of the EPA, actually prepared figures showing it would only cost U.S. Steel 94¢ per worker per day, or 75¢ per ton of steel, to resume polluting. He even offered to negotiate a lower fine. To no avail. U.S. Steel went right on obeying the law.

So much for the EPA. Next, two other agencies crush the theory that the federal government is the greatest protector of our natural resources.

• Around June 1976 it was revealed that the Bureau of Land Management and the National Park Service had both approved uranium mining leases for the Exxon Corporation *in the Grand Canyon*. The Interior Department was very embarrassed about it. Why? Because *neither agency had required Exxon to file environmental impact statements*. Bureaucratic procedures had been violated. *First,* file an environmental impact statement, *then* tear up the Grand Canyon.

Indifference to human needs is one of those qualities of bureaucracy that made it into the dictionary, so we hardly need supply examples here. We see it all too often as it is. The indifference results from those ever-present rules, rules, rules. To the bureaucrat, the rules are more important than the people they are meant to serve.

There are, however, times when indifference grows into something far more sinister, a callous disregard for all human values. The following is a case of this. I was shocked when I first heard of it, and I still find it shocking. One would not believe things like this go on, but they do.

> • In the summer of 1977, the Environmental Protection Agency issued a new policy order to the effect that it would no longer fund or approve tests, *on humans,* of substances known to cause cancer. The new policy grew out of a disclosure that two years earlier, senior EPA officials had nearly succeeded in funding a test to feed Mexicans massive doses of a fungicide known to be carcinogenic. The policy order specifically reserved the right for the EPA to continue to conduct tests on humans of substances merely *suspected* of causing cancer.

How could senior government officials undertake such a horrifying scheme? What was on their minds? What sort of insane atmosphere is there deep inside the bureaucracy that tolerates experiments like this, much less carries them out? I have struggled to understand it, and cannot. If there is a bureaucratic logic to it, it's the logic of Auschwitz.

Bureaucrats call themselves "civil servants," but it should be increasingly clear that they are in business to help themselves — " and pretty freely, too," as the Fairy Queen says in Gilbert and Sullivan's *Iolanthe.* This helps explain why noble-sounding endeavors like the "war on poverty" never work. Here are two examples among many.

> • The Office of Economic Opportunity announced that it spends 81% of its budget on overhead — that is, on itself instead of on the poor.

> • "(AP) A federal job placement program for welfare recipients cut public assistance payments by $400 million last year, but all but $22 million of the savings was gobbled up by the cost of running the program, the Labor Department says." Score: Bureaucrats, plus $378 million. Welfare recipients, minus $400 million.

When the bureaucrats aren't helping themselves, their relatives, friends, associates, and contractors may be. Sometimes it's legal . . .

> • The Department of Health, Education, and Welfare ruled that the practice of officials of the National Institute of Drug Abuse awarding millions of dollars in contracts to their relatives and friends is not illegal, but does give a "substantial appearance of impropriety."

More often it's just plain graft, the camp follower of every bureaucratic scheme. Kickbacks, payoffs, account padding, ghost employees, undelivered goods, phony contracts, welfare frauds — the opportunities are endless. Every week of two, it seems, we read about another case of corruption or scandal. The food stamp program is bilked out of $600 million a year, according to a GAO report. HEW admitted misplacing $6 or $7 billion one year — it wasn't sure quite how much — much of it due to fraud and abuse. The General Services Administration was found to be ridden with graft from top to bottom, and its top administrators were fired. This sort of thing is well known, and we needn't dwell on it.

Not as well understood, unfortunately, is the other side of this coin — the corrupting influence bureaucracy has on American life. And it seems the more "idealistic" a program starts out, the more corruption it spreads. Consider the Summer Foods Service Program, which provided $160 million for lunches for needy children. The lunches were purchased from food management companies, and distributed through some 2,000 churches and charitable organizations. Now, who would steal food from poor kids? Read on.

> • "U.S. PROBING CHILDREN'S FOOD PLAN. Millions Believed Diverted From Lunches For Needy . . .
> "Justice and Agriculture Department investigators have

found evidence that the government may have been defrauded of millions of dollars by food management companies that provide the free lunches . . .

"[The] alleged fraud in the summer feeding program . . . included theft of food, substandard food, kickbacks, price-fixing, adult use of food intended for children and the dumping of extra food for which the government had paid.

". . . the FBI is investigating allegations that in some cases food suppliers agreed to kick back a portion of the over-charges to the sponsoring (religious or charitable) group . . .

"In one Atlanta case, according to FBI documents, children were regularly served only a quarter glass of milk but were given a full glass on the day federal inspectors were expected.

"In another case in Dublin, Ga., a preacher used his church as a day-care center, charged the government $16,384 for feeding children in June, 1970, but spent only $3,662 for their meals. He fabricated invoices to get reimbursed.

"In South Carolina, a pastor collected $6,986 to cover costs of $1,767, with most of the money spent on ineligible children . . ."

— From a *Washington Post* story

Programs that spread corruption among religious and charitable groups, that even tempt clergymen to steal, cannot be healthy. Yet this sort of result is all but unavoidable. Unless the program becomes an embarrass-ment, as this one did, the bureaucrats don't much care. It isn't their money being stolen, or their children being cheated. Their auditing procedures are too ineffectual to stop it anyway, even when rigorously applied, which is seldom the case.

  • A GAO study of 34 federal agencies found that only two, the Smithsonian Institution and the Interior Department, were in compliance with government audit rules.

Paperwork, forms, red tape — is the bureaucracy bent on annoying us to death?

  • In 1975, filling out federal forms was estimated to cost citizens and businesses $40 billion and 130 million man-hours a year. In a bold effort to reduce this burden, the government created a Commission on Federal Paperwork, which will undertake a two-year study of the problem.

Right. And file its report in sextuplicate. Here is what they came up with.

- "(AP) Americans most needing the help of government may be the least able to complete the forms required to get that help, the Federal Commission of Paperwork says.

  "Needy Americans complete more than 500 million federal forms each year, the commission found. Millions more forms are completed at the state and local level.

  "It may take the execution of as many as 60 separate forms to obtain . . . assistance, and a not atypical 10-year-old case was found to contain over 700 documents.

  "The commission quoted an April 1977 report of the Office of Management and Budget, which said individuals submit 231,211,159 responses annually requiring 65,643,952 hours to complete."

Very impressive. But one may be properly suspicious of such exact figures. One thing I've found is that nothing about the federal government ever comes up, believably, in exact figures, at least in recent years. Nobody even knows for sure how many bureaus, agencies, departments, subdepartments, subagencies, commissions, etc. it really has, or how much they spend, or how many different forms they use, much less how much time Americans spend filling them out. Ask "how much" or "how many" about anything in the government, and there is only one answer: "more than the human mind can comprehend."

Occasionally, agencies do try to make a dent in the paperwork problem.

- By a herculean effort, the Environmental Protection Agency managed to reduce one of its forms to a single page. But it had to provide a 90-page instruction book for filling out the form.

Just remember this: without all the information it gets from the forms and paperwork, how could the bureaucracy maintain its reputation for meddling?

Bureaus have to live with their own red tape and rules. Nothing is more amusing than one bureau meddling with another.

> • HEW higher-ups sent this message down to the rank and file: "Please do not water the plants in your office. They are under the maintenance contract and will be taken care of properly."

> • Citing Federal Property Management regulations, the GSA changed the locks on bureaucrats' bathrooms, to keep out bureaucrats with unsufficient rank.

> • "Rules-minded investigators found some lower-level transportation officials had more office windows than regulations allow. They went in to cover up two windows but were driven off by gales of laughter."
>
> — *The Wall Street Journal*

Sometimes innocent victims get caught in the crossfire when a couple of bureaus meddle with each other.

> • OSHA ordered a Massachusetts supermarket to put a nonskid floor in its workspace. The Agriculture Department made the market take it out again, and put in a tile floor for sanitation.

Bureaucrats habitually conduct their business in a strange and somewhat threatening foreign language, sometimes called Bureaucratese. This complicates every problem in dealing with the bureaucracy, especially the forms and paperwork, into a bilingual nightmare.

Granted, every trade and every profession has its own jargon, mine not least. But Bureaucratese is in a class by itself. I suspect that bureaucrats use it deliberately, to separate the "ins" from the "outs," and to keep the "outs" from understanding what really goes on in the bureaucracy. I also suspect that fluency in Bureaucratese is the key to the Treasury. Here are a few of my favorite specimens.

- Jimmy Carter described his plan for cities as one "to strengthen linkages among macro-economic sectoral place-oriented economies."

- Trying to get reports written in plain English, the Interstate Commerce Commission formed a "Zero-Base Gobbledygook Committee." You can judge its success by trying to figure out what a zero-base gobbledygook committee is, in plain English.

- Examples of U.S. government publications for sale: "78S, Horse Bots, How to Combat Them, Rev. 1973. 7 P. il. A. 1.35:450/4 S/NO100-02787." Another hot number, "59S, Supplement to Digest and Index of Published Decisions of the Assistant Secretary of Labor for Labor-Management Relations Pursuant to Executive Order 11491, as amended July 1, 1972 through December 31, 1972. 1973. 189 pp. L. 1.151/3:972/ supp. S/N 2900-00177." And my favorite, "82S, Rats, Let's Get Rid of Them . . . . Most people probably prefer to avoid a long-term relationship with a rat . . . . Rev. 1968. 8 p. il. 1 49.4:22/2. S/N 2410-00022." (And only 10¢).

Government language can be and is used to deceive. No outsider would have guessed that "A Bill to amend Part III of Subchapter O of the Internal Revenue Code of 1954" was in fact a measure to give tax relief to the Hilton Hotel chain.

One last quality about bureaucracy that is not well recognized, and ought to be, is that every federal agency and bureau is a police agency. The bureau's rules are meaningless unless it can enforce them, so every one has its own "compliance" or "enforcement" section — its own police force. Most have their own judges as well. Bureaus thus represent all three branches of government. They can make law, enforce it, and try and punish offenders, all in their own bailiwick.

Crime is seldom a laughing matter, but some of the

"crimes" that result from bureaucratic rules get simply ludicrous.

- Three Texans bringing corn shucks from Mexico to make tamales were arrested for smuggling. The corn shucks didn't meet federal corn shuck sanitation standards.

- A 26-year-old woman caught swimming nude in Baker Hot Springs National Park refused to dress and was immediately arrested because she "had no identification at that time."

- Bruce's Restaurant in Tyler, Texas, was raided by seven uniformed and armed officers who suspected that Bruce was selling crappies rather than catfish. Scooping fish bones and remains off plates as evidence, the officers arrested Bruce and his patrons, and hauled them off to a justice of the peace, where all were fined. "They came in here with those big guns and made the waitresses cry," said Bruce.

- High drama at sea one dark night. A U.S. customs helicopter swoops down on suspected criminal activity. Two suspects flee in a speedboat. The customs agents radio for help. Local officials send another chopper and a speedboat. A wild three-hour chase follows, during which the suspects ram a U.S. Coast Guard cutter that has joined the pursuit. Drug smugglers, of course? Not at all. The two were suspected of raking clams in waters that, according to federal regulations, were too polluted for clamming.

This concludes my review of federal bureaucracy in all its finery. You may have read a thousand stories like these, and yet when the next one comes along, you never cease to wonder: how could anyone be so boneheaded, slow, meddlesome, inconsiderate, weird?

It seems clear enough that the authors of the bureaucratic state, back in the New Deal days, never wondered about it. They had no serious experience with bureaucratic ways, and so didn't really know what sort of monster they created. There is no excuse, however, for the more recent architects of bureaucracy. The "yea" votes in Congress know full well that every time they create a new bureau, they are creating more bureaucratic headaches for America. But they say we, the people, demand it, and deny all responsibility. The fact is, they are fully and directly responsible; but they have a point.

The problem will persist as long as you and I, a majority of Americans, shirk our responsibilities and turn our problems over to the government for solution.

We should know by now that the government cannot solve our problems. It has no resources whatsoever that it did not take from us in the first place. And much of what it takes, it keeps. We think, or at least some people think, that we can unload our problems on somebody else. Then we end up with far more problems than we had to begin with. The "solutions" are forced on us, and we see them as boneheaded, slow, inflexible, inconsiderate, and weird.

And they are. You will have seen by now that bureaucrats work in a wholly different way from the rest of us. The difference is fundamental, going down to bedrock principles. Either we handle our affairs through free and voluntary association, or we turn them over to the bureaucrats, and have them handled with coercive rules and regulations. Those are really our only two choices. They are opposites and yield opposite results. Through free association, we produce what we need to survive and prosper. Under bureaucracy, we get rules upon rules telling what we can and cannot do. Bureaucracy produces nothing. Under bureaucracy we will, finally, starve.

Are there any common threads running through our experience with bureaucracy? I find three. First, all bureaucratic influence is based on its rules and regulations, rather than on what is sensible or economic. Second, all bureaucratic actions are imposed by force or threat of force, rather than being freely chosen. You and I are in the best position to decide how to manage our affairs, yet we are not permitted to. The bureaucracy, knowing little or nothing about it, does it for us. The point was explicit in Fascist Italy, which was plastered with posters of Mussolini with the caption, "He Will Decide." That is precisely what bureaucracy is all about.

The last common thread is taxes. Bureaucrats do not produce; they take. Everything they take comes off your table and mine. And what they take costs us more than food, clothing, and shelter — all the necessities of life — put together. Not counting any military spending, the current cost of federal bureaucracy is around $3,000 for every person in America. Little babies, people in nursing homes, everyone. Many of us would have trouble believing this, because it's far more than is deducted from our paychecks for income taxes and social security. But it's true. Rich people aren't paying your taxes for you, despite all the well-advertised "soak the rich" plans. You pay them, for the most part indirectly. Everything you buy or rent is marked up scores and hundreds of times to pay taxes. The money you bring home is marked down scores or hundreds of times to pay taxes. Inflation, which is nothing more than creating money, is a federal monopoly and another federal tax. You pay it in the higher price of goods and services. The bureaucrats spend it. Does your family budget allow $60 per person per week for feeding federal bureaucrats? Can you afford it? Let's hope so, because that's what bureaucracy costs you.

II

HOW BUREAUCRACY WORKS

There are [only] two methods for the conduct of affairs within the frame of human society, i.e., peaceful cooperation among men. One is bureaucratic management, the other is profit management.

It is well known that profit management is highly unpopular in our age. People are anxious to substitute all-round planning by a central authority . . . for the supremacy of the consumers as operative in the market economy. But at the same time the same people severely blame the shortcomings of bureaucratism. They do not see that in clamoring for the suppression of profit management they themselves are asking for more and more bureaucracy, even for full bureaucratization of every sphere of human affairs.

— Ludwig von Mises, *Bureaucracy*

It is easy to identify bureaucracy from its handiwork. When we see the perverse or wasteful or boneheaded results of some government boondoggle, we know instantly that the bureaucrats have been busy. But this only tells us what bureaucracy is doing, not what it really is. So we must ask: Just what is this thing we call bureaucracy? What are the qualities that set it apart from other human undertakings?

The answers to these questions are surprisingly difficult to come by. With bureaucracy intruding so heavily in our lives, you'd think it would be under the microscope of a thousand articles and studies. Instead, it seems to be largely taken for granted, its basic nature little known to us. Ask a dozen political science professors to define it and I doubt that one could do so with precision. We can note that the word literally means "rule by bureau," but this doesn't tell us much. Or we can accept the dictionary definition that it is "the body of non-elected officials of the government." This again is too vague. To define bureaucracy by the "laws" of its operation, as some do, is to describe the symptoms, not the disease.

It appears that we'll have to work through to an accurate definition of bureaucracy on our own. It is most important to our correct understanding of bureaucracy and its consequences. We're in no position to criticize it if we can't even define it.

After much investigation, I believe that bureaucracy is best defined by identifying its causes, the conditions that create it. I find three. These three conditions give rise to all bureaucracy, are always present wherever it is found, and interlock to give it its highly distinctive character. What surprises me about this finding is that the whole bureaucratic stew reduces to only three defining qualities. I would have thought there would be more. Indeed, I can rattle off a score of uniquely bureaucratic characteristics that are nowhere to be found outside the asylum. The more important of these bear discussion later on. But all of them derive from the essential nature of bureaucracy; they do not cause it.

For a working definition, let's just say that bureaucracy is the organized activity that results when the three conditions are met. Not yet satisfactory, but its meaning will be fleshed out as we discuss those conditions.

Before we begin, I must mention two other findings. First, bureaucracy is a definite thing, a system with inherent, consistent, and recognizable qualities. That is, we are dealing with just one thing, not many, not shapeless goo. In fact, bureaucracy exists in every country on earth, and it is remarkably similar in form and function wherever it is found. It is common to all forms of government and cuts across all cultural lines. Even the passage of vast amounts of time seems to affect it little. A career bureaucrat under the ancient emperors of China or pharaohs of Egypt would be completely bewildered by modern life, but — given a new suit of clothes and a briefing — would feel quite at home in today's IRS or FDA.

Second, bureaucracy can only be understood in contrast to its opposite and only alternative, private economic actions. If all the world were directed by bureaucratic principles — not that this is possible — we would not know that bureaucracy existed. It is the more familiar ways of doing things in private life that give us a yardstick to identify and analyze the workings of bureaucracy.

I use the term "private economic actions" here in its broadest sense, to mean all uncoerced — and uncoercive — human action. I specifically want to include all personal, family and other private matters, exchanges, and consumption of goods, services, and labor. The distinction is important because I will argue that bureaucracy is inherently helpless to manage any of these matters and has absolutely no business trying. This whole vast area of life is governed by other, nonbureaucratic rules, simple, few in number, and moral in nature. It is the area where conscience and individual choice must be supreme. That moral law works has been abundantly shown by history and needs no defense here. That bureaucratic alternatives do *not* work should be equally clear to everybody, except perhaps to the last cultists of Marxian ideals, who will not see the suffering of the abused masses in the socialist paradises they helped to create. It takes an iron will — and an iron stomach — not to see the universal failure of bureaucratic dictation.

* * *

The first step toward understanding bureaucracy is to see where it comes from. This we can pinpoint. All government bureaus originated in the same way. Their source is invariably *an extension of coercive government controls into private life.*

Notice that the form of government under which this occurs is irrelevant. It makes no difference at all whether the new government controls result from a law duly enacted by a constitutional legislative body, or are decreed by a Hitler. All that matters is that the sovereign state is expanding its power into some area of life that was previously private.

Now, as a practical matter, the supreme authority, the lawmaker, whether it be a dictator, a soviet, or a parliament, cannot personally oversee the execution and administration of the new law. The supreme authorities have other responsibilities, and besides, the job would be much too big and complicated for them to handle. In this country, Congress is constitutionally forbidden to put its own laws into effect, since that is an executive, not a legislative, function. In any case, the job must be delegated to an appropriate deputy or agency.

Consequently, when Congress extends federal controls into our private lives, it creates, in the same law, a new federal agency to administer them. And thus a new bureau is born. Little laws create little bureaus, big laws big ones. But in all cases the enlargement of government power produces a corresponding enlargement of the bureaucracy and its power. When you ask the government to do a favor, you get a bureau. (I only wish the interest groups that plead for special favors and protections, which invariably extend government controls, were aware that they are creating a monster.)

This is the first of the three defining qualities that set bureaucracy apart from other human enterprises: *All bureaucracy is empowered by, and is the executor of, coercive government controls.*

Some may immediately object here that bureaucracy infects private institutions such as business, labor organizations, schools, foundations, and so on. This is certainly true. But it is true *only to the extent* that these institutions are protected by government coercion. All the institutions mentioned are indeed so protected, in their charters, in subsidies, in favored tax treatment, and in other protective legislation. Thus they are, in varying degree, creatures of the government, the soil in which bureaucracy can take root and thrive.

On the other hand, bureaucracy in private settings is severely limited in its resources by economic processes, and has only limited and indirect access to coercive protections. No private institution operates, as real bureaus do, only with the tool of compulsion. Thus the private version is watered down and puny in comparison. It is a serious error to lump private and governmental bureaucracy together as if they were the same thing. They aren't. Only government bureaus wield the coercive power that is the mainspring of bureaucracy.

A word about what I mean by "coercive." It refers to the use, or threatened use, of force to compel people to behave in a given way. Coercion is the one central feature of all government sovereignty. Governments have, and in theory are supposed to have, a monopoly on coercion. All government undertakings are based on compulsion. All private coercion — that is, all cases where one person uses force to compel another to surrender property or do his bidding — are criminal. This is as it should be. Yet compulsion, governmental as well as private, is the most dangerous of instruments, and is all too easily extended into areas where it does not belong. We should never seek to run a farm or a factory on the same coercive principles that are needed to run a police station. Yet that is precisely what we are doing when we seek, or accede to, government controls over business, labor, churches, schools, and other obviously private areas of life. The controls are then administered by a bureaucracy that is coercive in nature, and we experience all the economic ills that result from using compulsion where it does not belong. And more often than not, we end up wondering what went wrong. The answer is that we should not have put cops in charge of our farms and factories.

The Founding Fathers were acutely aware of where such abuses of power could lead, and wrote the Constitution precisely to *limit* federal power. The Federal Government was permitted the few legislative powers specified in the Constitution, and no more. All other rights and powers were reserved for the several states and for the people. The Founding Fathers believed, as I do, that the rightful powers of government are essentially negative or defensive in nature: those needed for national defense and for the security of citizens' lives and property. That the Constitution has since been "reinterpreted" to permit any sort of federal meddling is a total perversion of the Founders' purposes, and a tragedy.

I raise these points to stress that it is the coercive nature of bureaucracy that gives rein to all of its mischief. Conversely, if an organization does not have coercive power, it is not bureaucratic. If bureaucrats had no power to compel us to do as they wished, they would be no factor in our lives.

The second defining quality of bureaucracy flows from the axiom that sovereigns *never* surrender their powers voluntarily. There may be some exception to this rule somewhere in history, but I have not found it. The logic of government is to seek or seize new powers and grow. It is rare indeed when a government can be pressured into yielding an ounce of power or inch of soil by any means less than superior armed force.[1]

This axiom has a direct and immediate effect on the way a new bureau is established by Congress. On the one hand, Congress must delegate power to the bureau; on the other, it must retain its absolute sovereignty *over* the bureau. Thus the bureau must be made to execute the will of Congress and remain answerable to Congress. Obviously it cannot be allowed to do as it pleases or take what funds it pleases from the Treasury. It is but an agency or deputy of higher authority.

Congress solves this dilemma the only way it can, by ruling the bureau. Its instruments to do this are the budget and the Rulebook. If each new law comes equipped with a shiny new bureau, each bureau comes

---

[1] One of the few cases of this on record was the reform movement of the 19th century, which resulted in the wholesale repeal of protectionist laws in Europe. These mercantilist laws regulated every detail of domestic and foreign trade, and made every country in Europe an island unto itself. Competition from free Americans did them in. The repeal movement was spurred by the invention of the speedy American clipper ship, which all but wiped British merchant shipping, lifeblood of that island nation, off the seas. The British then had an impossible choice: make war on us (hopeless), compete, or starve. In desperation, they chose to compete, and in 1849 repealed the Navigation Acts, destroying trade barriers and opening their ports. In a few years, Britain's own Aberdeen Clippers were among the best — some, like the *Cutty Sark* are still legendary — and the new freedom ushered in a time of enormous prosperity. The repeal movement and its benefits quickly spread to mainland Europe, smashing trade barriers. Despite the obvious benefits that resulted, Parliament and the other European legislative bodies divested their powers only grudgingly and under intense pressure.

equipped with a rulebook. The rules detail the government's wishes and instructions as to how the bureau is to administer the new law. *The supreme duty of every bureau is to follow the rules.* Arguably, the bureau's *only* duty is to follow the rules.

This is the second distinguishing feature of bureaucracy, and its implications are many. Here, for instance, we find the reason that bureaucracy is so notoriously rigid and unresponsive. What else can it be, if its duty is to the rulebooks? It cannot serve the particular needs of those it is pleased to call its "clients." Rather, the clients' needs must be pushed or pulled — or abandoned — according to how they fit the agency's rules.

The rulebook approach also explains why the very best agency head can do little better than the worst. Neither has the discretion to make sweeping changes. What discretion they have covers only internal agency matters or minor rules; they cannot alter the agency's mission or charter.

Similarly, many other annoying features of bureaucracy can be traced to the rulebook. Yet bear in mind: there is no alternative. The bureau itself must be controlled from above, and the rulebook is the only way to do so. The bureau's spending must also be controlled from above, for the bureau always can — and always will — argue that it could do a better job if only it had more money.

Citizens unaware of the bureau's duty to the rulebook may easily be deceived about its purposes. They may assume, for instance, that the purpose of the Environmental Protection Agency is to protect the environment. In fact, the EPA's mission is to obey its rules, and it cannot protect the environment any better than its rules allow. If Congress chances to devise rules that do protect the environment at an acceptable cost (which would take a miracle), fine. But if Congress goofs and makes rules that will lead to fouling the water and the air, the EPA is equally bound to *them*, and it becomes, in effect, the Environmental Destruction Agency. Results of this sort, quite the opposite of what the law was *intended* to do, not only occur, but do so with appalling regularity. This is no coincidence.

The rulebook approach does not and cannot work. It is much too crude and clumsy; about as intelligent as trying to fine-tune your watch with a war-axe. It is not possible to devise rules, however complicated, that can apprehend the infinite diversity and subtlety of human affairs. Nor can rules deal with the fact that people don't like to be pushed around and will go to great lengths to avoid them. In other words, no matter how well-intended or clever a rule may be, people will simply change their behavior and make it obsolete or worse than useless. Nor can rules, so laboriously drawn up in the dawdling, play-it-safe world of government, ever catch up to the fast pace of real life. For these reasons the rulebook approach inevitably, and usually in short order, produces results contrary to those the legislators intended. The failure of the first rule leads to the promulgation of another, and another, and another, with widening social damage, until we find ourselves trapped on a one-way trip to totalitarian government. This is not just theory but the clear fact of recent history.

There is more. Rules corrupt. In a way we will explore later, every rule creates economic privilege for some and an unjust disadvantage for others. This in itself is corrupt, and it creates endless temptations for more corruption, by those who seek privilege, and by those in the bureaucracy who create it with the force of the law. A better breeding ground for injustice and social resentments, by those who have been cheated, can hardly be conceived. Worse, it offers a tailor-made excuse for almost everyone to join in the corruption. After all, "I've been cheated and I want to get even" or "Everyone else is getting theirs, why shouldn't I get mine?" Not only do the rules create a widening vicious circle of more rules, they spread the attitude that crime pays. I'm convinced this attitude, caused by the abuse of government power, is one reason crime rates are soaring.

We see all these results, call them perverse, and blame the bureaucracy. Then we demand more of the same; more rules, more protection, more government, more bureaucracy. This is the road to oblivion, the one traveled by every civilization before us. We *must* understand that the danger lies in giving the government tasks it cannot possibly perform; that its only tool, compulsion — the rulebook, the gun — is wrong in private economic affairs. Compulsion may be used to deter crime, but it is helpless to manage economic affairs. Compulsion cannot grow our food or make our clothing or build our homes. Those who must produce at gunpoint are slaves. No slave society ever gets enough to eat. Millions upon millions of people today know this from bitter experience. If we learn nothing from this, if we ignore Mr. Jefferson's warning, if we simply go on doing what we have been doing, there is no way we can avoid the same fate for ourselves.

The third and last defining characteristic of bureaucracy is that it is wholly political in nature and operated exclusively in a nonmarket, not-for-profit setting. The real importance of this lies less in what bureaucracy is than in what it lacks, so let me rephrase it this way: *All bureaucracy functions wholly outside the marketplace; no market-determined price exists for its services, and there is no objective relationship between its revenues and its expenditures.*

In describing a bureau as "wholly political," I refer not to mere partisan politics, but to its core nature as a public or governmental body. This nature is completely different from, and unrelated to, anything in the economic world. There is no "bureaucratic" market. Bureaus do not sell, and customers do not buy, services in the market sense. This means they have no economic mechanisms or market information about their own actions. Not only are their aims and operations different from any business, but also their structure and management. We will explore this in a later chapter.

As political bodies, bureaus operate only in a political context and respond only to political power. No possible reform can turn them into economic vehicles, or give them economic tools, or make them respond to economic stimuli and disciplines. None of this is in their nature, any more than it is in the nature of private business to serve police functions with compulsory methods. The two are worlds apart and will always be so.

These simple facts have implications that range far indeed. They mark, in effect, the absolute divorce between the bureaucracy and economic activity of any sort. What they mean is that bureaucracy, irremediably, is denied the tools of rational economic management. What they imply is that all central government economic planning will fail.

Moreover, these findings can be confirmed by the full weight of economic science. We may well be satisfied, intuitively, that the police have no business meddling in business matters (or vice versa), and that, by extension, neither do bureaucrats armed with the same powers as the police. The intuitive case is not in itself conclusive, however. The reply will inevitably be made that our argument speaks only for selfish, private interests, whereas bureaucratic interventions serve an overriding public interest. This is nonsense, and simply represents totalitarian pleading. There is no supreme being called the Nation or the Public or Society that has "interests" apart from and superior to our collective interests as private citizens (which is what the market represents). The Russians have a proverb, one hundred heads do not make One Great Head. Or as Frank Chodorov reminded us, society *are* people; take away the people and their interests, and you are not left with some being called society that has its own interests. Every plea you hear for some bureaucratic intervention in the economy "in the public interest" is in fact a scheme to serve selfish special interests by giving more power to the State. Even if it isn't intended that way, it will turn out that way, Milton Friedman has noted, as if led by an "invisible hand" to do so. The proof of this lies in economic law, which we will turn to presently.

* * *

I said at the outset of this chapter that we could not very well criticize bureaucracy unless we understood it. With that in mind, let us briefly review our findings so far.

Bureaucracy, we find, is a worldwide phenomenon (and universally detested). It is common to all forms of government and political systems, and has been since the beginning of recorded history. It is a simple, identifiable method of organizing human effort, and its form appears to have changed only in minor detail over thousands of years.

We find further that bureaucracy is defined by three qualities that are always present in its functioning, and that interlock to give it its distinctive character. First, all bureaucracy is created by, and is charged with executing, coercive government controls. Coercion, the use or threatened use of force, is its *only* tool. It is entirely financed by coercion as well. Second, bureaucracy is responsible to, and only to, higher government authority. Its supreme duty is to follow the rules that authority establishes for it. As a legal body, it must follow legal rules, and cannot be given any significant discretion in its activity. It is not responsive to the citizenry and cannot be controlled by them except through indirect and almost inaccessible political channels. Third, bureaucracy is a purely political (i.e., governmental) body. It functions wholly outside the economic marketplace. No relationship exists between its services and its income, so its performance cannot be objectively judged in dollar terms. It is, in other words, completely removed from, and different than, economic or other private activity. It has no tools to manage economic activity. Conversely, an organization that does not possess all three of these qualities cannot be considered part of the bureaucracy. Such a group may have some characteristics that we regard as "bureaucratic," but only insofar as it enjoys protections or privileges from the State, and always in a far smaller degree than the State's own bureaus.

It cannot be overstressed that we cannot fully understand bureaucracy except in contrast to its opposite, private forms. Only two methods exist to organize productive human activity. One is coercive, governmental, and dictated by State authorities: this is the bureaucratic method. The other is free, private, and voluntary, and is directed by all consumers (even those in other countries): this is the profit method. We call the latter capitalism, or the free market economy. These are the only choices we have, and they are polar opposites, alien to each other, oil and water. A system that mixes them is at war with itself. Each of these forms of organizing, the bureaucratic method and the profit method, has its place, but neither can handle the work of the other. Any effort to employ either where it does not belong can only cause harm and waste and destruction. History is rich in examples of whole civilizations that have died trying to impose the bureaucratic method where it was bound to fail.

Given these considerations, it is apparent that it is by no means as easy to criticize bureaucracy as we might have supposed.

For instance, we may dismiss out of hand the complaint heard occasionally, that bureaucracy is some sort of undemocratic element within government. It is nothing of the sort. It is the muscle tissue of government, the handmaiden of political authority.

No more cogent is it to blame the excesses of bureaucrats on the fact that they are not elected. It is hardly practical to elect millions of bureaucrats, but even if we did, there would be little or no difference in bureaucratic functioning. It is the job that makes the bureaucrat what he is, not how he got there. His job is to follow the rules. For the same reason, little blame accrues to "bad" administrators for the failings of their bureaus. Replacing them will scarcely ease the problems. The rules give bureau chiefs little discretion to make changes, and even if they had more freedom of action, they could not change the basic nature of the bureau or its mission. Reformers who call for putting crack businessmen in charge of bureaus miss the point entirely. The businessman can't use his administrative expertise or hard-nosed business sense in a bureau: the rules don't allow it. Moreover, the bureau does not serve business purposes, cannot use business tools, and must deal with problems unknown to business. Putting a businessman in charge simply turns him into a bureaucrat.

We cannot criticize bureaucracy for being "unresponsive." It does respond — but not to you and me. It responds to its boss, higher government authority (mainly Congress), to its budget and to its rules. The only control that we, the citizenry, have over bureaucracy is the electoral process, notably selecting a Congress.

This is so oblique and slow as to be all but meaningless. Congress itself cannot change the nature of its rulebook control over bureaus. It can create or eliminate bureaus, but it can't change their spots.

Criticizing a bureau for being inefficient and wasteful is like accusing an elephant of being large. *Of course* it is wasteful. We have a market economy to handle everything that must be done efficiently. All the rest, the things that cannot be done efficiently, the things that are inherently wasteful, are left to the bureaucracy. A bureau cannot be anything but wasteful. It has no natural checks on its revenues or spending. It has no efficient economic tools at its disposal. All of its built-in incentives are to waste. The more it can squander, the more power it gets, and power is the pot of gold for all political enterprises. These are important matters, and we will have a closer look at them later on.

I do not even share the widespread sentiment that bureaucracy is an "evil," although much of its handiwork is undeniably vicious and destructive. Bureaucracy is merely a method of organizing certain activities, and is neither good nor evil in itself. What we perceive as evil in it is the political power and ambition behind it — the extension of totalitarian government measures into what should be private areas of our lives. Note with care what I am saying, for there are few of us indeed in private life who have not added to this evil in demanding things we are not entitled to — competitive advantages in business or labor, enforced by government police power; telling others what they can read or say or own, where they can build or buy, how they run their business; demanding "welfare" with money somebody else earned and needed. Turning these, or a thousand other illegitimate demands, over to power-hungry politicians all but guarantees the triumph of totalitarianism. Who is to blame for the evil results — you, or the bureaucracy set up to commit the evil you demand?

What, then, *is* wrong with bureaucracy? Just one thing, in my opinion: its misuse, or application to the wrong tasks. For reasons we will explore more fully, bureaucracy should never be applied to private or economic purposes. In these areas it always does harm. Unless economic law fails me, this is an absolute rule. Bureaucracy cannot settle or manage any private matter; never can it rule in matters of conscience or morality. Bureaucracy is equally helpless to regulate economics. It cannot be used to create or control any economic enterprise. In an economic setting it is worse than an idiot; it is blind, deaf, and brakeless. Its only weapon, compulsion, is utterly helpless to improve our well-being or enrich our lives.

Please notice: I do not say bureaucracy is useless. There are tasks for which compulsion is not only the right tool but the only tool. The obvious examples are national defense and police protection of our lives and property. The Army is a textbook case of bureaucracy at work. It must be managed by bureaucratic techniques. Free market techniques in the military are out of the question. There is no way we can support national defense by peddling it in mail order catalogues. Neither can we deter the criminal by pleading with him. At some point compulsion is necessary. Imagine the spectacle of a cop saying to the fleeing thief, "Stop, pretty please, in the name of the law!"

But by the same token, it is just as ridiculous, if not more so, to tell the farmer or businessman or laborer that he must produce this and not that, at dictated rates, under such-and-such conditions. This is the nature of all bureaucratic intervention in the economy, and it is certain to do more harm than good. We simply cannot run a grocery store the same way we run the Pentagon.

Once we recognize that bureaucracy and the marketplace offer alternative and opposite methods of management, each with its own rightful place, we can draw a sharp line between the areas where each should be used. If a job truly requires compulsion, and few do, it is the exclusive province of government and bureaus. Economic methods cannot get it done. If the job is private or economic, it is the exclusive province of voluntary associations and the market. Bureaucratic methods cannot get it done.

Am I really saying that the government has no business intervening to protect us from snake oil peddlers, unsafe working conditions, unfair labor practices, pollution, monopoly, and all the rest of it? You bet I am! Given a fair chance and a little time, the market will solve all of these problems, as market economists have made clear. And interventions won't. The bureaucratic "solution" actually tends to create more of these problems; certainly it creates monopoly, privilege, and injustice. But I would go further than this: I believe those governmental chores that do require compulsion are extremely limited. I believe that we could use private methods far more than we do to deter crime, and even to help with national defense. There are endless cases on record of private businesses successfully handling what some might think a purely governmental function — a fire department, for example. It is, in other words, our national habit to rely on government and bureaucracy to do a great deal that it cannot and should not do. In almost every case private firms could do the same jobs better, faster, and cheaper. If you are skeptical of this, look at your tax bill.

Many will find this hard to swallow, I know. Most if not all of us have our own favored interventions. And we can always find noble reasons for minding other people's business. Suppose we conjure up the image of some gaunt, helpless child toiling long hours in a coal mine or sweatshop.[2] Our sense of fair play, of humanity, is outraged, and we say, "there oughta be a law." And soon there is. Then another, and another . . . . Demagogues and reformers can very easily play on such emotions, on our generosity, to demand more power for the central government. And if you oppose them, they will paint you to be a child abuser. But it is they who are creating injustice and hurting the child. If the reformer had advanced the same proposition in different words, it wouldn't have sounded so good: "Let's pass a law taking jobs away from children who desperately need them to keep from starving." This is in fact what happened historically when the child labor laws were passed. Such evil side effects always follow when government coercion is misused.

The definitive answer to all such meddling is that it

---

[2]There are perfectly respectable cases to be made for sweatshops or child labor, but you won't find them in today's textbooks or learned journals. Nobel laureate Milton Friedman cheerfully defends sweat shops as way stations that helped immigrants get established in this country. He knows: his mother got her start here working in one. Of course the wages were low, but the jobs did pay something, and nobody considered it permanent employment. As for child labor, what is so terrible about letting children take jobs, as long as they are not literally forced to? Nothing. On the contrary, we who are parents rejoice when our children learn how to work and earn their way. The pathetic cases from long ago that you read about in some history texts were not nearly as bad as painted. The children often got their only hot meal of the day on the job, and they did make something. A job at "wretched" wages is miles better than none, if you need it. It is interesting indeed that the drive to abolish child labor was spearheaded by a clothing maker's union whose members at times *competed* with those poor children for jobs. So much for their "humanitarian" motives. The union is still around and still bragging about it.

But what really happened? Laws were passed that took away the children's right to make a living. And other laws were passed to "crack down" on sweat shops, and those stole jobs from penniless immigrants. By this process, the unionists took the jobs from the poorest and neediest among us, and called it humanitarianism! And they didn't tell you that the low wages for child and sweatshop labor reduced the prices of goods for customers who, in those times, were struggling too.

does not work; that it causes more harm than good. The case against intervention has been made in detail by Mises and others, and is beyond the scope of this book. But it's simply a matter of common sense. The government has nothing to give. What it "gives" to you must first be confiscated from somebody else. That is unfair. If it "reforms," it is overruling the arrangements people have voluntarily worked out for themselves. If it creates legal privilege for some, it creates injustice for those now at a disadvantage. Add to this plain sense the fact that the government pays itself lavishly to dispense these questionable services, and it becomes clear why all bureaucratic interventions cost more than they are worth. Their collective cost at this point is mind-numbing; well over a trillion dollars a year at all levels of government. That is, in nominal dollars, three times as much *every day* as the federal government spent during the first fifteen presidential administrations — in seventy-odd years from George Washington to the Civil War.

The cost of intervention is much greater than dollars. The interventions tend to destroy both the individual's responsibility for self-protection ("let Uncle do it") and the market's own, remarkable self-policing mechanisms, which offer far greater protections to consumers than any bureaucratic rules ever devised. Worse, all interventions tend to establish, by coercion, vested interests, monopoly, and social parasitism. And all, because coercion can create privilege and unfair advantage, are vastly more susceptible to graft and corruption than are any private abuses. Bureaucracy does not save us from business or labor corruption, it creates corruption. All interventions infringe on property rights, and so tend to weaken and finally destroy the economic mechanisms on which our very survival depends. And, finally, all interventions expand police powers and transform a free society into a totalitarian state. That, in outline, is the case against bureaucratic meddling in private life.

What does it take to learn this answer? How many civilizations must crumble from overweening government and bureaucratism? How much more suffering will the collectivists inflict? How many more millions of political murders will they commit to try to make their "system" work?

No, I have no trouble sticking to the principle here. Keep bureaucracy where it belongs, and get rid of every bit of it that intervenes in economic or private affairs. Cut off its funds, root it out, kill it dead!

III

BUREAUCRACY AND ENTERPRISE: IRRECONCILABLE OPPOSITES

It [the State] has taken on a vast mass of new duties and responsibilities; it has spread out its powers until they penetrate to every act of the citizen, however secret; it has begun to throw around its operations the high dignity and impeccability of a State religion; its agents become a separate and superior caste, with authority to bind and loose, and their thumbs in every pot. But it still remains, as it was in the beginning, the common enemy of all well-disposed, industrious and decent men.

— H.L. Mencken (1926)

It is unfortunately none too well understood that, just as the State has no money of its own, so it has no power of its own. All the power it has is what society gives it, plus what it confiscates from time to time on one pretext or another; there is no other source from which State power can be drawn. Therefore every assumption of State power, by gift or seizure, leaves society with so much less power; there is never, nor can be, any strengthening of State power without a corresponding and roughly equivalent depletion of social power.

— Albert Jay Nock (1935)

We have examined the principal qualities that define bureaucracy and set it apart from private life. Here we are going to march boldly into the enemy camp for a closer look, to see just what makes a bureau tick. We will examine its structure, policies and everyday operations, and even peek at its books. In looking at these details, we can see how starkly they differ from what we do in our own lives, and the way we get things done. I trust you will find the contrasts informative — and alarming.

It is ever useful to "know thine enemy," and doubly so in this case. For one, understanding how bureaucrats operate may allow you and me, as individuals, to stay out of their clutches. Americans are pretty adept at evading bureaucrats already, and I'm all for it, if nothing immoral is involved. Nobody says you have to volunteer for serfdom. Merely knowing that bureaucracy, like electricity, follows the path of least resistance, has let many a nimble individual get out of the way.

Second, and more important, if enough of us see clearly the great harm that bureaucratization is doing to America, we can put a stop to it. One election may not achieve this result, but for the first time in two generations the political winds are blowing our way. This gives me confidence that the decision is still ours, and that we can do much, much more. The first step is learning all we can about the nature of the beast.

As we've seen, a bureau is purely a political body, the creature and servant of State authority. I'm sure you are only too familiar with the aroma of politics. Yet unless you've been there, it's hard to grasp how thoroughly political modes pervade and shape every detail within a bureau, and give it a character altogether unlike anything in our private experience. Scrutinize bureaucratic operations at any point and you will find them effectively the opposite of the economic alternatives. The one operates on force, the other on persuasion; the one serves the government, the other serves the people; the one confiscates, the other earns. These differences are unbridgeable, and carry over into such pedestrian matters as pay scales, working conditions and hours, promotions, and so on. Public and private organizations do not even keep their books the same way, and could not if they wanted to. The implications of this are much deeper than one might guess.

These differences will reveal why the bureaucrat, in his political setting, is ever the klutz trying to direct economic matters outside his bailiwick. But let's be clear right now that this is not because bureaucrats are stupider or, somehow, different from other people. They aren't. It may be argued that bureaucratic careers attract some kinds of people more than others. But it must be conceded that bureaucrats as a group are quite as normal and intelligent as anybody else. They do not charge off to work in the morning with a vision of how to create some monumental boondoggle.[1] When they come home at night they do not tax their neighbors or inspect their kitchens for safety compliance. Neither is it true that the perverse effects of bureaucracy can be attributed to the bureaucrats' particular incompetence or dishonesty or indifference. It tends to be just the other way around: the better they do their jobs, the more

---

[1]Albert Jay Nock thought otherwise, at least as far as politicians are concerned, and loosed upon them some of his choicest scorn:..."[c]am paign promises are merely another name for thimblerigging. The workaday practice of politics has been invariably opportunist" and "exerts its most powerful attraction upon an extremely low and sharp-set type of individual." He then noted, "Henry George made some very keen comments upon the almost incredible degradation that he saw taking place progressively in the personnel of the State's service . . . As for the federal House of Representatives and the state legislative bodies, they must be seen to be believed." "The general upshot of all this," he concluded, "is that we see politicians of all schools and stripes behaving with the obscene depravity of degenerate children; like the loose-footed gangs that infest the railway-yards and purlieus of gas-houses, each group tries to circumvent another with respect to the fruit accruing to acts of public mischief."

One doubts that this may be said of bureaucrats, or all of them anyway, but Nock certainly has the politicians' number.

perverse the results. And if an unusually high proportion of bureaucrats raid the cookie jar or engage in questionable practices, that just goes with the territory. In short, it is the job itself, not the bureaucrat who holds it, that is the problem.

Every bureaucratic job must, as a matter of law, conform to the rules, and execute the purposes, established by higher government authority. The first definition, we recall, is that: Bureaucracy is always an instrument and executor of coercive government power. Consider the implications.

Bureaucracy itself is never the supreme authority. It does not establish its own purposes, set policy, or act on its own. It is but a deputy, albeit one backed by the full force and power of the government. Its job — to borrow Nock's terminology — is to enhance State power at the expense of social power. This may correctly be likened to a military operation in hostile territory. The point is not lost within the bureau, which comes to regard the private sector it is invading, and business in particular, as the enemy. Indeed, bureaucracy is notorious for its hostility toward commerce, and rarely seems to comprehend that the private production process it is attacking is the only source of sustenance for all of us and for itself.

What is especially noteworthy here is the *lack of any true purpose in the bureau.* As a legal deputy, the bureau may not set its own compass. Its orders come down from above, and its job is to follow them to the letter. Its book of rules may cover the minutest detail, but it cannot provide *purpose.* Nor can purpose be discovered in the bureau's self-interest; what interest has it, in serving the wishes of higher authority, except to be a bigger hog slopping at a wider trough? Each new bureau, it's true, comes equipped with a statement of purpose; but this is merely a legal definition, and of necessity a vaguely worded one, describing where the bureau is to operate.

The best one can say is that this provides some direction; but it does not provide a purpose nor even a sense of purpose. The lowliest clerk or toiler in private business knows exactly what the organization is trying to do. The bureau chief, for all his savvy, has no such certitude about his own agency, for it has no true purpose and is ultimately ruled by politics.

From all this a sense of aimlessness filters down through the bureaucratic ranks. The individual bureaucrat is, in effect, often asked to define and create his own work, filing endless reports on what he has done, or is doing, or intends to do, or whatever he can think of to report. The reports become the work — what else is there? We on the outside joke about bureaucrats writing each other memos, but in the purposeless environment of the bureau, those memos are a triumph of concrete achievement.

It is, I grant, very difficult for those of us on the outside to accept that the bureaucratic job, for all its high-sounding statements, has no real purpose. Yet it is so, and crucial to our understanding. Perhaps you can get more of the flavor from this letter written by a perceptive and intelligent friend of mine, while he was serving some years ago with a federal agency I shall not name:

> The work here poses no great challenges, except perhaps defining what the work is. [Our agency] is charged with managing [a bigger agency's] finances to break even. This it cannot possibly do. The whole thing is run by statutes, and the law prohibits any kind of rational management. Everything is pre-Adam Smith. So there is answered one question of burning interest to the libertarian theorist — can you work for reform from within? Answer: no. Next question, can you cut the waste out of government? Answer: no. All that's holy in the bureaucracy demands ever-more waste. Government *is* waste. Maybe you could kill a whole agency, but you couldn't squeeze the fat out of it. And if you did kill it, all but the newest employees would be guaranteed a comparable job in other agencies.

> . . . . it's all just paper shuffling and serving time. I'm serious that grown men cannot even define their own jobs or functions. They spend endless hours writing reports on what their "activities" will be (if they get around to it), or writing useless "studies" or just reading newspapers. It must weigh on some hearts besides mine that there is no real work, no purpose, that it's all serving time for fat salaries and pensions. The people are intelligent, personable, friendly (no problem there); but unfulfilled. Nobody ever comes early, stays late, or gets worked up over an assignment. Lights are *supposed* to be left on, and desks left in a littered mess, to give the appearance of activity.
>
> The [agency] just completed a . . . case — a "real" assignment. Here functions were more clearly defined and work was quite hectic (even a bit of overtime). The thing was important in having big money implications [for the principals]. It was also ridiculous in its statutory methods and net conclusions — pure fantasyland. Unless I read things wrong, the people here welcome these "cases" because it makes them feel as if they are gainfully employed. We won't have another for some time — so back to paper shuffling . . .

There is the view from inside. The person who wrote this, I am permitted to say, abandoned a cushy salary and an all-but-guaranteed future to return to more purposeful, if less remunerative, work in the private world. But only a handful ever manage this, and that is a large part of our problem. Could you force yourself to give up a handsome salary — one that your family is accustomed to, counts on, and spends, if only mentally — for snoozing at a desk, when the alternative is working your tail off for less? That is the problem with escaping the bureaucracy, and under the circumstances, we can hardly be critical of those who fail.

If we are to find an answer here, it must begin with putting the bureaucrat back into perspective. This will not be easy. For two generations, government interventions have been glorified, in the press, from the pulpit, in scholarly works. In this, the bureaucrat has been glorified to a status far greater than he deserves. Yet we have among us a much older and deeper tradition that may still put matters right. For most of our existence as a nation, and for seven generations of colonial life before that, the bureaucrat enjoyed no such esteem. Until the New Deal years, our concept of the federal employee was that of a *civil servant* — a harmless if underpaid drudge who could perform the simple services of government. For many generations of Americans, this was a harmless if slightly tainted thing to do — if one could do nothing better. It is only in the last fifty years that government has been elevated from employer of last resort to something glamorous and special — employer of millions! Spender of billions! And now the "civil servant" waxes fat, paid far too much with taxes extracted from the productive people, but doing nothing of any greater importance than before: the Servant become the Master.

Where, in the American experience in liberty, did it ever say that we should be ruled by bureaucrats? To restore sanity, we must restore the right concept of government service *as service.* This almost by definition would rule out overweening bureaucracy and would restore to the federal service what small purpose it has, beyond justice and defense, in a free society. Bureaucracy should not be an attractive occupation, and without its present prestige and high pay, it would not be.

But perhaps I am mistaken; perhaps I exaggerate the importance of human freedom. Perhaps the bureaucrat should enjoy his exalted status and more, while we the people submit to our status as lowly subjects. I think this is tommyrot, but men thought wise occasionally argue this way. Surely one way we can dispose of the argument is to compare the bureaucratic mode, point by point, with the way we do things in our own lives.

"Social power," *purpose, and profit.* Literally all of the

productive effort in our lives begins with our own personal efforts, and the expenditure of our life energy. There is no other source of energy than what we willingly give of ourselves. This effort may be channeled into voluntary associations or commercial enterprises that multiply our efforts, but only so long as no coercion enters the equation. The sum of our efforts is what Nock called social power. I believe what hopes we have for the present and the future lie precisely here. Certainly, personal efforts and the unhindered market have proven themselves to be an amazing engine of prosperity and a powerful force for peace. Not only do voluntary and economic actions sustain us in bodily needs, they give us the means and the time to pursue noneconomic ends and spiritual enrichment. (Has a bureaucrat ever spoken to you about matters of the spirit?) I ask you: Is this not what we want in life? And have we not the right to choose our own future? In freedom we create and we choose. Under bureaucracy, somebody else chooses, eventually a Mussolini, and not in our interests.

It is in the private sphere, too, that we find real purpose, the same so lacking in bureaucracy. Indeed, it is so obvious that we scarcely notice. In our business activities, we know exactly what we are trying to do, which is exactly what the bureaucrat does not know. Business has concrete function. Farming is farming. One makes cars, or sells insurance, or cuts hair: the intent is always clear. Never in unhindered business do we suffer the malady common to bureaucracy that we have no real idea what we are doing. In business, we serve those who would buy our services for their own betterment, and we must do so in a way that is so efficient and effective that we can make a living at it: make a profit.

Profit, for all its repugnance to some ears, is the objective of all who would serve others. In Mises' definition, the "market economy is that system of social cooperation and division of labor that is based on private ownership of the means of production." Its characteristic feature, he goes on, is free enterprise. "The object of every enterpriser, whether businessman or farmer, is to make profit."

It is the never-ending search for success, for profit, that gives business enterprise the purpose and direction lacking in a bureau. And it does so in a socially valuable way, for in the unhindered and competitive marketplace, you must serve others efficiently in order to profit. People serving people: this is social cooperation, without any of the negative implications of being forced to do so by State authority.

In any personal economic enterprise or business, you have to give value to get value. You have to please. This shapes the character of everything you do. Under bureaucracy, you needn't give value for anything or please anybody. This equally shapes the character of the enterprise. Given this fact of life, we needn't be surprised that the former must be honest and that the latter invariably becomes corrupt and larcenous.

The marketplace. The free market is by definition the sum of all uncoerced exchanges. Markets can be as simple as kids trading baseball cards, or as complex as a computerized commodity exchange with worldwide ties. But they all share the key element that the market is free and open, that no coercion is used or threatened or produced by the deal. All legitimate business takes place in markets so defined.

Let's be clear: protection deals cooked up between politicians and business or labor are not a part of the free market. They are part of the bureaucratic world, and corrupt. The fact is, bureaucracy has neither goods nor services to sell in the open market. What it does have to "sell" is a line of privilege and protection, backed by State coercion. Often this is lawful — if thoroughly dishonest —as in licensing what people have every right to do anyway, or subsidizing business, or protecting trade unions. But lawful or not, forms of the same protection rackets inevitably proceed in the bureaucratic mode: selling lucrative government contracts for lucrative kickbacks, selling monopolies in labor or business, and literally thousands of other types of corruption.

Exchanges. In legitimate business, all exchanges are two-sided, value given for value received. All parties to an exchange enter it voluntarily, and all do so expecting to better their condition by doing so. All parties to an exchange expect to profit from it, otherwise they will not agree to it. In short, everybody comes out ahead, each according to his own scale of values and priorities. This process of free exchange thus facilitates the continual distribution of capital, goods, and labor from those who have less use for them to those who have more. On this fact the modern world is built. Without this, we would have no way to assign the resources and responsibilities needed for economic enterprise. With it, we build a world in which people on welfare can in many regards enjoy a higher standard of living than the kings of old.

Bureaus, on the other hand, derive all their revenues from one-way transactions that are not exchanges at all. Bureaus simply confiscate, through State power, the production of others, without compensation. In such transfers, only one party profits; the other gets soaked. This gives the injured party a perfect incentive *not* to produce. Why bother if you're just going to get ripped off again? The net effect of the transfer, then, is not zero but a net loss of productivity and human wellbeing. Private crime produces the same disincentive — armed robbery on a street corner, for instance — but constitutes such a small percentage of involuntary transfers that its economic damage is minimal. Private crime accounts for no more than 3% of all the one-way transfers, probably less. The rest is bureaucracy and government in general, and the damage is staggering. Government at all levels sucks up something more than 40% of all our productivity through involuntary transfers (as opposed to about 1% from private crime). There is hardly a business in the country that could sustain the loss of 40% of its output without facing bankruptcy in a week. Yet that is the rate of confiscation we, as supposedly free citizens, are forced to bear in order to support the bureaucracy. Small wonder we all struggle and can't get ahead!

The cost of government at all levels today is around a *trillion* dollars a year — a million millions — all of it, of course, confiscated. That works out to about $4,500 per person, or $18,000 a year for a family of four. The smaller part of this — much the smaller part — goes for national defense and other State functions most of us regard as legitimate. But most pays for bureaucracy. Without this bureaucratic exaction, families would be keeping $12,000, $15,000, $18,000 more of their income than they do now. Is bureaucracy worth that much to you? Are you willing to have it go on doing what it is doing, at such a cost to you? If you were offered, say, a $15,000 per year pay increase in exchange for not having a bureaucrat on hand in Washington to "solve" your problems for you, would you take it?

This is an essential question in addressing bureaucracy, but by no means the only one. No one knows how much more than this bureaucracy costs you in its disincentive effect; it could be that your "pay raise" for doing without it would be $20,000 or $30,000 a year. Nor can anybody calculate, in dollar terms, the cost of freedom and opportunity lost, due to bureaucratic high-handedness. But even without a final dollar figure, you can surely judge whether you are getting your money's worth from bureaucracy. Think about it.

Economic protections. There are, of course, ways to rip people off in business: selling "gold" bricks, mail order scams, snake oil, and the like. But turning a quick profit with such methods is less attractive than it might seem to larcenous minds, and certainly is not without risk. Scams pose scant problems in an unhindered market where consumers are enlightened by the old doctrine of "caveat emptor" — let the buyer beware. (This warning is, if anything, more useful today when we supposedly rely on bureaucrats and lawyers to protect us; the wise consumer will ever apply it.) In any event, the price we pay for an occasional unwary purchase of a gold brick is very small change compared to the price we pay for bureaucrats to protect us from the con artists. And the protection we get from that quarter is worse than useless. Bureaucrats don't prevent swindles; they license them, and take a cut of the action.

The overwhelming majority of businesses are, and must be, straight arrow, for the real road to wealth is satisfying the customer and gaining dependable, predictable repeat business. The businessman who gains a reputation for honest dealing is also the one who can make his business calculations most accurately, hence enhance his profits and expand his business. Conversely, if a person gets a reputation for dishonesty or swindling in business — and one incident will do it — that person is going to get run out of business and probably out of town. The open market thus produces a strong bias for honesty. This extends into every facet: honest weight, honest ingredients, honest quality, and yes, honest advertising. The penalty for dishonesty can be overnight ruin and a lifetime stigma. Consumers pay your bills, and if you deceive or misserve them and lose their trust, your business is finished. Economists thus argue that the market, if it is not hampered by State interventions, offers consumers infinitely more protection than laws or bureaus or any remedy the Nader movement ever dreamed of.

The argument that officials of the State can protect consumers through interventions and regulations was destroyed by Adam Smith more than two centuries ago, and has never been tenable in economic theory. All such measures are anti-market, and all, by their nature, tend to create monopoly for some and disadvantage for others. That is why corrupt businesses and industries seek to be regulated in the first place, and scream bloody murder at the threat of deregulation, a phenomenon we have seen often in the past few years. *Of course* they hate deregulation: it will cost them their bureaucratically protected monopoly and force them to face the disciplines of the market: competition and the need to serve customers efficiently. Nobody wept more bitterly about deregulating the oil industry than the "consumer advocates"; many and loud were their warnings that this would raise fuel prices for consumers. And it did for a few months, as the market sorted itself out. Then the price of oil started dropping like a stone. Within a year the so-called "energy crisis" that was so frightening to some —mainly people who detest the market — turned into a worldwide oil glut that is breaking the power of OPEC. The market works. Bureaucratic controls don't.

The real question, then, is one you never hear from the "consumer advocates": who or what will protect us from bureaucracy? There are no economic checks or disciplines whatsoever on bureaucratic activities. Utterly insulated from economic risk or loss, bureaus keep right on growing, no matter how badly or wastefully they perform; no matter that they have been obsolete for a decade or a century in what they do. Not only do we pay their bills in taxes, we pay in increased consumer prices in every economic activity they regulate. Bureaucratic controls invariably destroy market efficiency, so increase the cost of goods. The net effect is that we get more bureaucracy and less to eat for our dollar. Some claim that this is "protection" for the consumer, but you'd spend a lot less buying the Brooklyn Bridge every week.

Marketing. Business has no instrument except persuasion to promote sales, and truth is much the best persuader. For this reason, the enterpriser is generally at pains to make sure that everything is on the up and up. Indeed, it is common for the enterpriser to take all the risks of an exchange by offering potential customers demonstrations, samples, free trials, and so on. You can't do that unless you are honest in your dealings and confident in your product.

It is too silly for serious thought, but just imagine for a moment what life might be like if bureaucracy had to be as honest as businesses. What if bureaucrats had to offer free samples of their famous handiwork? Back up their claims? Offer a money-back guarantee if not 100% satisfied? If bureaucracy had to use any of these everyday business practices concerning its own efforts, it would be good-bye bureaucracy before sunset.

Alas, it can never be. Bureaucracy doesn't even have anything to sell, and needn't please a soul with its services. It doesn't have to sell itself, except to Congress. And if it did, it could make any claim it pleased without fear of running afoul of laws against fraud and deception. It is exempt from those; the laws apply only to private businesses and individuals, not to the government itself. Yet, I believe that, in their secret hearts, bureaucrats want to be liked by the rest of us. Certainly they go on and on and on trying to sell us on their virtues and compassion. It is a hopeless enterprise, but they keep trying. The claims they make for themselves range from ludicrous to outrageous to gross fraud. They claim to dispense justice and fight poverty and protect the rights of workers, minorities, women, consumers — what utter bilge. Any private operator who tried to peddle worthless securities would end up in prison. The feds do it every day, selling what they fraudulently call "savings" bonds. Some "savings." The interest on the bonds is less than the inflation rate, so the return is a net loss. Moreover, it is the government itself that sucks the value out of the bonds by inflating the money supply — a nifty swindle that no private con man can match. Inflation is a government monopoly. Where are the so-called "consumer advocates" when millions of Americans are bilked by such bureaucratic schemes? Where are the advocates of truth in advertising when the FDA claims it is protecting your health or the EPA claims it is protecting the environment? Truth is the first casualty of bureaucratic promotions. Bureaucrats are not the sort of folks I'd buy a used car from.

Bookkeeping. Here, as I intimated earlier, we find a most interesting distinction between bureaucracy and business. They keep their books differently. They have to. The methods of modern accountancy are not open to bureaucracy.

Business, and only business, uses a double-entry system. This simply accounts the fact that every transaction produces both a plus and a minus. In a simple case, if a merchant sells an item, it puts a plus in his cash account and a minus in his inventory. Double-entry bookkeeping is so familiar and commonplace to the businessman that he never gives it proper appreciation; yet it is indispensable to the modern world. As Mises noted, it took a great poet, Goethe, to recognize the true value of this method. Double-entry bookkeeping, Goethe said, is "one of the finest inventions of the human mind." Why? Because it permits the businessman to weigh the success and prospects of his enterprise at any time without bogging down in a million details.

This is indeed genius, and here we have the heart and

soul of economic calculation, the tool that makes economic progress possible; the tool, lacking which, bureaucratic central planning must fail. This is quite a claim for a mere method of accounting, but it is this method and no other that reflects the reality of economic exchanges. Without it, there can be no objective assessment of myriad factors of production, of the signals of the market, of success, risk, and failure. Without it, there is no economic planning. We are fortunate that the enterpriser does have this tool and can use it to make the needed calculations and keep track of any division or aspect of business — all but instantaneously in these days of the computer.

What does bureaucracy have in comparison? Nothing. It uses a form of single-entry books, and a strained sort at that. One entry over here to record revenues, i.e., appropriations from Congress. Another over there to account expenditures. And no economic relationship whatsoever between the one and the other. Bureaucracy isn't selling anything: the next credit in its cash account is not matched by a corresponding debit in inventory or any other account. About the only useful information the bureau chief can get from this is whether his agency is in the black this fiscal year. Any reasonably bright paperboy can get better information than that from his accounts.

Management. On the surface it might appear that a businessman directing a commercial enterprise and a bureau chief directing a government agency would have comparable if not interchangeable jobs. The slightest investigation, however, will show that nothing like this is the case.

Even their job titles suggest that private and public managers are different breeds. In business, titles tend to be crisp and functional, reflecting purposeful positions: President, Chief Executive Officer, Division Manager, Plant Foreman.

Bureau titles say nothing, and are something of a joke. The head of a bureau is always an "administrator." A what? One who "administers." One who administers what? Who knows? — the bureau. If the bureau has cabinet rank, the chief is a "secretary." Does that convey more than "administrator"? Under these chiefs are a welter of Assistants and Deputies and Assistant Deputies and Deputy Assistants, and assistant Deputy Assistants and . . . ad infinitum. What do all these people do? They help the administrator administer.

Ask the administrator what his agency does, and you will at once be awash in bureaucratese: It administers. Evaluates. Studies. Investigates. Determines. Develops. Coordinates. Revises. Manages. Recommends. Disseminates. Implements. Formulates. Expedites. Mush words every one, lacking in all sense of *doing* anything, precisely because the agency *isn't* doing anything, as other people understand the word "doing." Whatever it is doing, it is too obscure to be defined in the words of the working world, and the administrator himself is never quite sure of these matters or whether they are worthwhile.

It is the whole question of purpose again. Everybody in business knows what he is there for. The company makes widgets, we are trying to make a profit doing so, and my responsibility is ———, shipping clerk, division manager, chairman of the board.

This sense of things is lost to the aimless bureaucratic world, and grown men can spend their days writing memos about what they will do, and routing them around for other grown men to read.

Managerial responsibility. Any manager at any level of an enterprise in the open market can be entrusted with responsibility for his area with little more instruction than this: Make a profit. This is so because the manager's own interests coincide with those of the company. If he succeeds and makes a good profit, his own fortunes will improve. If he fails, the failure can be seen at once through the accounting of profit and loss. Then the manager will either get sacked or his division will be discontinued; either way he is out of a job. In other words, the manager's own success is inextricably linked to his performance on the job, and this is checked by accountancy. In these conditions, the owner or enterpriser or top officer can safely *divide and delegate responsibility* to his subordinates.

Responsibility can never be divided in the legal setting of a bureau. All responsibility is legally defined and firmly vested in an unbroken chain of command. But if all the responsibility is directed by the rules, what credit — or demerit — can accrue to the individual manager? Very little. If something goes wrong, who is responsible? Everybody blames the rules and passes the buck up the chain of command. If something goes right, everybody up the chain claims credit, deserved or not. What is everywhere lacking in this system is the *reality* of personal responsibility. In the rulebook world, real responsibility vanishes.

Managerial discretion. Discretionary action is the complement of responsibility, and the same considerations apply. The business manager can be trusted to act at his own discretion; the bureaucrat cannot.

It is very much in the interest of top business management to let its subordinates use discretion, without interference from above. The subordinate then bears full responsibility for his performance. If senior managers interfere, then they, not the subordinate, are responsible for the results. Since the managers' actions are both checked by accountancy and disciplined by market forces, they can be left to manage as they see fit. This, in turn, is often the impetus for highly creative efforts by the subordinates. People just seem to do better acting on their own understandings instead of conforming to dictated rules.

In contrast, very little discretion can be allowed anywhere in government service. Those who make the rules must live by the rules.

Wage structure. The ideal compensation in a market enterprise, in economic terms, would be exactly tied to one's productivity and profitability to the enterprise. That is, you would be rewarded for exactly how useful your efforts are. This is a system of *complete* opportunity and *no* wage protection. What you do is your responsibility: the harder you work, the better your output, the more you earn. Conversely, you have no excuse if you slack off or fail in some way; you earn less. Seldom, nowadays, do enterprisers employ this system as such, although piecework payment and sales work on a pure commission basis come close. Less precise is an hourly wage scale. Still more distant from the ideal are monthly or annual salaries.

Many workers and many employers prefer a less-than-ideal system that offers more protection and less pure opportunity. I cannot argue that they are mistaken. Many things can go wrong in business, and workers can suffer adversity through no fault of their own. I see no harm in voluntary employer-employee arrangements that spread the risks of misfortune in payment plans. If employees wish to work for the same wages, even though some are more productive than others, there's nothing wrong with it. The better workers must give up some of their opportunity, but the poorer, slower, or less lucky ones get a better shake.

As an economic matter, these are simple issues and easily understood; and in any case, compensation is always determined by the market. Unfortunately, the issues have been muddied by *political* concepts of compensation, often backed by political power. Such concepts tend to a sort of insane "compassion" and pay no attention at all to productivity or market forces. Here we encounter such lurid notions as a guaranteed annual income (which means the right to steal what somebody else earns) or "equal pay for comparable effort," a hot issue among the more zealous feminists, which treats all effort as if it were of equal value on the market, which it most assuredly is not. Less lurid but more harmful are the many contracts in force in "regulated" industries or in other areas of business or labor that are given monopoly status by bureaucratic intervention. In these areas, compensation plans take statist forms based on scale and seniority. Those so protected tend to be paid far more than their worth to the market. There is a price to be paid for this: widespread unemployment among less privileged workers, and competitive failure among the industries so "favored." The fatal flaw in all such arrangements is that you cannot cheat the market any more than you can fool Mother Nature. All will come to grief, and no police power can prevent it. We would be infinitely better off getting bureaucracy out of business and going back to voluntary compensation forms.

Compensation forms in the bureaucracy itself are totally divorced from economic reality. In the bureau, after all, there is no measure of performance; there is no way to judge success or failure; there is no productivity or profitability to tie compensation to; and there is no market to determine payment. Since it has no economic standards, the bureaucracy pays its own according to rank and seniority. What this has to do with the bureaucrats' value to society is — nothing. Since the bureaucracy can, in effect, help itself to as much money as it wishes (i.e., all the taxes the traffic will bear), its employees naturally tend to be wildly overpaid. If you had a license to steal, wouldn't you use it?

Promotion and job security. The economic standard for

advancement is increased value to the market. As you get better in your work and are worth more to your employer, you get paid more. If your employer goofs and fails to pay you more, you are free to move on to a position that does; and your former employer is penalized by losing your valuable services. In other words, in matters of promotion and job security, as with compensation, values are determined in the marketplace, and all the same considerations apply. It is precisely the freedom of the market that protects the employee from arbitrary decisions by his employer (and vice versa). From the give and take of the marketplace emerge precise standards of value. And from it also emerge different opportunities, so that you may always seek full value for your effort. As long as labor markets are free, in other words, your labor cannot be exploited by heartless capitalists acting individually or in concert. There are always plenty of honest businesses eager to get a competitive edge on those who engage in dubious employment practices.

Interestingly, the same factors offer a high degree of protection against all forms of personal discrimination, whether it be for racial, sexual, or whatever reasons. Your value on the market is not determined by race, creed, sex or personality; it is determined by your productivity. Even your crazy Uncle Jack is employable if he can do the job, and if his eccentricities are not disruptive. The single best friend for minorities, women, or others whose earnings lag behind the average is not legal remedy but a market of wide-open opportunity. A free market. If you've got the stuff, opportunity is what you need, not coercive protection. Protection doesn't make you any better. What you can and do contribute to the economy makes you better.

All of these considerations turn exactly upside down in bureaucratic employment. Where all is determined by the rules and no freedom exists, all decisions become arbitrary. Where there can be no standards of performance, advancement depends on — personality. Politics and personality. Merit cannot be recognized, because there is none in a measurable way; you have to kiss your way up the chain of command. In these matters bureaucratic practices resemble, and were in fact derived from, military organization, as we'll see in a later chapter. The distortions they cause are more fully discussed there.

Meanwhile, we are left to wonder: what appeal is there in a bureaucratic job that does not serve others; that does not pay according to merit; that does not have room for or even recognize achievement? Could you stand it? I'd go out of my skin. What *is* the attraction — the excessive pay? The sense of power, in being able to push people around with bureaucratic rules and interventions? Or is it just that bureaucracy today, as it always was, is the home for losers who can't make it in the real world? I wish I knew.

* * *

What I do know is that free enterprise and bureaucracy are worlds apart, irreconcilable, hostile, forever sundered. The character of each is fully shaped by its purpose, the one economic, the other political; the one social, the other antisocial and exploitative if uncontrolled.

Surely the ways of the one and the other should be clear enough by now so that we can assign each to its rightful place. Yet the story is older and more profound than we can imagine; let us suspend judgment as we consider the ancient and surprising origins of the bureaucratic problem.

IV

THE PRIMEVAL BUREAUCRACY

The State can have originated in no other way than through conquest and subjugation.

The State . . . is a social institution, forced by a victorious group of men on a defeated group, with the sole purpose of . . . the economic exploitation of the vanquished by the victors.

— Franz Oppenheimer

I now pose one of the less flaming academic questions of the day. In fact, I've never heard this issue raised at all in academic circles. Nevertheless, the answers I have found are both surprising and full of insight about the purpose and character of bureaucracy. The question is, *where did bureaucracy come from?*

Obviously, there was a time in the very distant past when bureaucracy did not exist, perhaps ten thousand years ago or more. The simple nature of earliest human communities would have ruled out the use of bureaucratic measures. The North American Indians never did develop any, or a State for that matter, possibly excepting a few fishing tribes in the Pacific Northwest. The same has been true elsewhere among certain kinds of peoples under certain conditions. But at some point, under some other conditions, an ancient people must have devised and perfected bureaucratic methods. Why? What were they doing that required coercive behavior? How did their situation differ from that of peoples who did not use coercion? These are matters worthy of reflection.

Even though ancient tribes left no written records, scholars have been largely successful in reconstructing how the various types lived. This is done in part with archaeological evidence, by observation of peoples still living in primitive conditions, through logical inference based on food supplies, location, climate, and similar factors. The same reasoning will show us the origins of bureaucracy.

We group the ancient peoples according to their main occupations. The principal types were hunter-foragers, grubbers (primitive peasant farmers), herdsmen, and fishermen. One of these had the honor of introducing bureaucracy into human affairs; but which? It would have had to be a tribe that engaged in some sort of violent action against other humans; this alone would explain the need for coercive organization. Thus, coercive measures are best explained by the emergence of a warlike tribe that learned to survive by plundering more peaceful peoples.

It is clear that neither the hunting nor the farming groups used systematic violence. Neither had any possessions or food supplies worth raiding. What can one peasant forcibly take from another that he doesn't already have? However, the herdsmen had a significant and valuable possession in their livestock. Surely it was tribes of herdsmen who first engaged in raids on each other, to steal stock. And in these skirmishes we have the first hint of the future Department of Health, Education, and Welfare. Talk about a living fossil!

Of course, raids for plunder are a far cry from systematic bureaucracy. Yet at heart they spring from the same impulse, and the seed had been planted. The next step was expanding the raids into wider areas, and clashes with other groups, in particular settled farm communities that had begun to prosper.

We can draw several inferences. For one, there must, by then, have been something to steal; otherwise the warrior tribes could not have gained by plunder. In other words, there already existed peaceful groups that were sufficiently civilized and settled to accumulate belongings of value. Archaeological evidence not only confirms this, but suggests that there was extensive trade among them, sometimes over astonishing distances. We may surmise that they had developed agriculture on good land, that they were tied to the land, that trade broadened their standard of living, and that they maintained communications with one another. The warrior herdsmen, in contrast, must have been rootless and nomadic, wandering from one target area to another. They were people of the plains and deserts, land sufficient for pasturage but not for farming. They were highly mobile and undoubtedly had domesticated horses or camels. They must also have put a lot of effort into developing weaponry. All the evidence suggests that the first warrior tribes emerged on the steppes of Central Asia, although other warrior groups have developed independently in similar conditions many times. Over and over, human violence has developed where prairie-land meets rich farmland; where nomads of the plains clash with settled farm communities.

In these skirmishes, the nomads have all the advantages. The meat and milk from their herds give them a better and more dependable food supply than farmers or hunters; their population thus increases faster. And individuals grow bigger and stronger on their protein-rich diet. Not for nothing did they become known as "hordes." Moreover, their mobility gives them a huge military advantage over settlements. They can strike at will, without fear of being pursued and counterattacked out in the endless prairies. If the settled communities resist successfully at first, the raids turn into a blood feud, and the nomads return again and again, in greater numbers, until they triumph. This is exactly how socio-historians reconstruct the events so long ago.

I would add one point — one of the greatest interest to us. One advantage the nomads did not enjoy was surprise; the settlements could communicate with each other. Thus, the nomads had to be better armed, better organized, and better fighters. They had to hone their military skills and organize themselves into disciplined fighting units. This organizing had to take coercive, bureaucratic forms, as it invariably does in military operations. In plain words, they turned themselves into an army. There is no possible way to do this with voluntary arrangements. Somebody has to take charge and give orders; others must obey orders. This creates rank and rulebook — a true bureaucratic system. *Here, I believe, is the genesis of all bureaucracy today,* in military organization in prehistoric times. And it must have occurred thousands of years before the invention of what we call government. There are still many evolutionary stages we must go through before we meet the first rulers, the pharaohs of Egypt.

What I am saying, very simply, is that bureaucracy was invented by marauding armies. It evolved as a necessity of military actions. A military unit can be organized no other way, as the first armies doubtless discovered.

Franz Oppenheimer, who quite literally wrote the book on these matters,[1] observed these necessities without recognizing them as the origin of bureaucracy. He wrote, "Hunters, it may be observed, work best alone

---

[1] *The State,* Bobbs-Merrill, 1914; originally published in German as *Der Staat.* Reissued in 1972 by Arno Press and the *New York Times,* New York, N.Y. Despite its wealth of scholarship, the book is lively and readable.

or in small groups. Herdsmen, on the other hand, move to the best advantage in a great train, in which each individual is best protected; and which is in every sense an armed expedition, where every stopping place becomes an armed camp. *Thus there is developed a science of tactical maneuvers, strict subordination, and firm discipline."* (My emphasis.) He then quotes Ratzel's observations of a nomad camp: "Everyone and everything here has a definite, traditional place; hence the speed and order in setting up and in breaking camp, . . . It is unheard of that any one without orders, or without the most pressing reason, should change his place." Such "disciplinary forces," it is noted, have existed "since most ancient times." There could hardly be a plainer picture of the nomads organized into a military force on bureaucratic principles.

What I, as a historian, find so interesting about all this, is that bureaucracy must have antedated government by millenia. We always associate bureaucracy with government, and rightly so. Yet here we see it before there was any such thing as government. The irresistible conclusion is that *the State was invented by bureaucrats,* and not the other way around! All the evidence supports this conclusion.

It's plain that nomad raids on bottomland settlements went on for many centuries before any formal State structure began to emerge. The first marauder tribes did not see any value in the lives of their victims. That is, they did not regard people they were attacking as having any economic value to them. They would simply swoop down on a settlement, take the women, livestock and anything else worth stealing, and kill everybody else. This is State-like activity, to be sure, but much too crude for any long-term success.

What we see here in raw contrast — millenia before the pharaohs — are the only two ways men can survive:

either they can produce, or they can steal what others produce. Oppenheimer, defined these as the "economic means" and the "political means," respectively. Over a vast period, the "economic means," or production, developed into what we call the free market, or capitalism; the "political means," or plunder, into the State. In this early, brutal stage, the contrast between them is particularly illuminating. Only a system of production allows all men to survive and prosper. In a system of violence and plunder, some must die for others to live. If all were to live by plunder, all would die, for nothing would be produced. The plunder system is thus a sort of cannibalism, with part of the human race feeding off the rest. This is still so, but the system has been immensely refined.

The first refinement in the system was of monumental importance to human affairs. It was simply this: the raiders learned to exploit their victims' toil and property, instead of just slaughtering them. The nomad bureaucrat learned that a hewn tree produces no fruit and that a dead peasant produces no goods. The warrior tribes learned that grubbers and hunters could be more useful to them alive than dead. It was a revolutionary discovery, and changed life forever. This was the genesis of the State. It was the birth of history itself, which from the beginning has been the record of State activities. And ever since, history has been marked by the continuous conflict between the peaceful producers and the organized State; between one group of plunderers warring with another over the spoils.

According to one rather romantic insight, the first State was created when some nameless nomad warrior enslaved his victim instead of killing him. And this goes to the heart of the matter, although the process was much more complicated. Certainly, slavery was, and in a sense still is, the central purpose of the State. The State was originally organized for no other purpose than to control slaves. Oppenheimer, by no means a hostile observer and normally calm in his scholarship, was moved to emphasize the point sharply: "The ownership of *slaves*! The nomad is the inventor of slavery, and thereby has created the seedling of the State, the first economic exploitation of man by man."

Slavery is not profitable unless the slaves can produce more than they cost. This is not the case in primitive situations. It occurs only after a certain amount of economic development, an accumulation of wealth that can only be increased by using outside labor in the form of slaves. This point is reached first by nomads, the size of whose herds depends on available labor. Herds must be constantly tended, guarded, and moved to fresh pasturage. The tribe can therefore increase its herds only as much as its supply of labor permits. After a time it must find additional herders, and for this it turns to slavery. The first slaves were impressed to increase nomad herds. It stands to reason that the tribe's existing military self-discipline, its bureaucratic system, could be and was immediately adapted to the task of controlling these slaves. Slaves take orders. The tribal leaders had long since learned how to give orders and have them enforced. More accurate is the surmise that the State was actually created when slaves came under the control of the nomad military bureaucracy. And at this point, it really is possible to discern the future HHS (formerly HEW), the U.S. Department of Health and Human Services.

Only one step remains to turn the fledgling State into a form we would recognize, however primitive and feudal. This is the addition of a defined *territory*. It develops over a long period of the nomad raids against the civilized settlements at the edge of the plains. The nomads are not only growing stronger by using slavery;

they are also getting more and more taste for the "political means" as they learn the ways of power and command. Their wanderings take them over a specific area, quite literally their own hunting ground. The raids in this area become a sort of harvest. The peasant communities, at the same time, learn, in innumerable defeats, that resistance to the heavily armed nomads is impossible. "But," Oppenheimer writes, "the peasantry do not flee. The peasant is attached to his ground, and has been used to regular work. He remains, yields to subjection, and pays tribute to his conqueror; *that is the genesis of the land states in the old world.*" (Original emphasis) Indeed so, for now the tribe, or part of it, must settle in the area, and begin the regular collection of tribute — taxes, in our time — and attending to the other duties of statehood. The nomads have abandoned their economic role as herdsmen for a new and wholly political job. They own the territory *and* its people.

It was by this process that the Hyksos herdsmen overran and subjugated Egypt to create the first "authenticated" State nearly four thousand years ago.[2] Innumerable examples have been observed since, and may still be observed today. It has occurred among all races and kinds of people when the right conditions were present. It occurs among fishing people, or sea nomads, as readily as among land nomads, and for the same reasons; all such peoples became sea robbers or pirates if there was something to steal within their range. (In

---

[2]This was by no means the *first* State in Egypt; merely the first in which the process of conquest was observed and written down in a historical record. The pharaonic State was by this time already very ancient, some two millenia old, in Egypt. It was the Eighteenth Dynasty of pharaohs that finally defeated the Hyksos, around 1570 B.C. The invasion gives a clear picture of the military supremacy of the nomads. The Hyksos introduced the horse and horse-drawn chariot to Egypt. They also used compound bows that were unknown in Egypt, and introduced the general use of bronze.

fact, some land nomads, for instance the Scythians, turned to sea piracy as soon as they learned how to sail.) It occurred in total isolation in the new world (Central America, Peru), even though the tribes had neither horses nor livestock. There can be no doubt that the State originates in violent conquest for the purpose of economic exploitation.

Yet, paradoxically, the more the State structure develops from its bloody origins, the more civilized it becomes, and the more it acts as a civilizing factor, at least in the early stages. This occurs because the conquering tribe and the conquered, formerly adversaries and of different stock, become master and slave with some interests in common. The economics of slavery also demands that the slave be allowed his subsistence, and from this develops the first public right.

As Oppenheimer explains it, when resistance ceases, the herdsman finds it "in his own interest (to let) the peasant live . . . The expedition of the herdsmen comes just as before, every member bristling with arms, but no longer intending nor expecting war and violent appropriation. The raiders burn and kill only so far as is necessary to enforce a wholesome respect, or to break an isolated resistance. But in general, principally in accordance with a developing customary right — the first germ of the development of all public law — the herdsman now appropriates only the surplus of the peasant. That is to say, he leaves the peasant his house, his gear and his provisions up to the next crop. . . . Great is the progress (in this advancement) . . . . The peasant thus obtains a semblance of *right* to the bare necessaries of life; so that it comes to be regarded as *wrong* to kill an unresisting man or to strip him of everything." From this beginning, better relations grow between the two groups: "Since the herdsmen no longer meet the peasants in combat only, they are likely now to grant a respectful request, or to remedy a well-grounded grievance." It is only a matter of time until the ruling tribe begins *protecting* its slaves from other raiders — the genesis of what we call national defense.

Oppenheimer calls this a "magnificent process of external amalgamation" and admiringly credits it with being the source of virtually all the good and great things we enjoy in our own times. "Although this is the beginning of all slavery," he writes, "it is at the same time the genesis of a higher form of society . . . ." He sees the developing State as the source of "nations and unions of nations . . . the concept of 'humanity' . . . the all-compromising love of humanity, of Christianity and Buddhism . . . nation and state, right, and higher economics . . . love and art, no less than state, justice and economics." He further likens the whole process to one of mankind growing up. The State "changes the half-playful occupations of men into strict methodic labor, and thus brings untold misery to innumerable generations yet born. Henceforth, these must eat their bread in the sweat of their brow, since the golden age of the free community of blood relations has been followed by the iron rule of state dominion. But the state, by discovering labor in its proper sense, starts in this world that force which alone can bring about the golden age on a much higher plane of ethical relations and of happiness for all. The state, to use Schiller's words, destroys the untutored happiness of the people while they were children, in order to bring them along a sad path of suffering to the conscious happiness of maturity." Well!

It certainly does not tax one's imagination to look at this amazing body of research and come up with totally different conclusions. What, one wonders, could be so bad about the "golden age" that preceded the State? Or about the "half-playful occupations of men" that preceded slavery, untold misery, and toiling "in the sweat of one's brow"? How is slavery "labor in its proper sense"? It takes no great skill with economics to realize that slavery is hopelessly inefficient. Is not all this toil simply the result of the many having to work harder to support their unproductive captors? Of course, and so it remains in this parasitic system. Nothing that the ancient conquerors did seems to me to produce "right." Before the coming of the herdsmen, the peasants had nothing to fear for their lives and property. What sort of "advance" is it if the conquering herdsmen give back some fraction of the rights the peasants had always enjoyed? I see little or nothing here that cannot be explained better by simply supposing the ancient nomads learned a more productive form of herding — using *people* as their stock. Of course they learned to care for their new herd and protect it from predators —what herdsman would not do as much for cattle? But herding it was, and herding it remains. I call it tax-herding. There is very little in the activities of HHS, or the Pentagon, or the Food and Drug Administration, that cannot be explained by a good manual on animal husbandry.

One keen observer who did in fact draw wholly different conclusions from Oppenheimer's researches was Albert Jay Nock. Nock got right to the point: he titled his little book *Our Enemy, the State*. Written in 1935, it is a classic, and is still in print.[3] We'll be referring to it later on in our discussion.

For now, our task is to see what lessons for today can be drawn from the violent and barbaric origins of bureaucracy so long ago. Or to put it another way, what

---

[3]*Our Enemy, the State;* William Morrow & Co., New York, 1935. Reissued by Arno Press and *The New York Times*, New York, 1972. No other book that emerged from the New Deal period came close to this one in grasping the long-term importance of the revolutionary changes then occurring. Nock was exactly on target, and his melancholy reflections are as important now as then.

use do we still have for our ten-thousand-year-old fossil friend, the bureaucrat? Do we really want our lives controlled by the living heir of plundering nomad hordes?

Perhaps you find the point far-fetched, but it isn't. The bureaucracy retains much of its military character to this day, in its missions as well as its structure. This may come as a surprise to many, but we cannot fully understand bureaucracy until we recognize its military side. It is no coincidence that as States and their bureaucratic apparatus increase in power and scope, they tend to become more and more militaristic, with a military dictatorship the end product. In this, they are merely reverting to their most ancient and purest form. We will turn to this next. The danger of bureaucratism taking a military form in this country is not to be taken lightly.

V

THE ETERNAL BUREAUCRAT

(Herbert) Spencer remarks the fact so notoriously common in our own experience, that when State power is applied to social purposes, its action is invariably "slow, stupid, extravagant, unadaptive, corrupt and obstructive." He devotes several paragraphs to each count, assembling a complete array of proof. When he ends, discussion ends; there is simply nothing to be said.

— Albert Jay Nock

On April 29, 1981, an ordinary day in the bureaucracy, the United States government spent $43,146,983 — over $43 million — for goggles.

— Related in *National Review* by James W. McClain, Jr.

We have traced the origins of bureaucracy among nomad armies in ancient times. One may reasonably wonder what this has to do with bureaucracy today. Many centuries have passed. Things have changed. Surely even in Washington, D.C., where all things are possible, there is a limited demand nowadays for nomad hordes.

Yet bureaucracy is still with us, and still doing business at the old stand, controlling and exploiting its prized herd of taxpayers. Perhaps things haven't changed quite as much as we'd suppose. Moreover, when we seek an example of bureaucracy at its purest, it would have to be in the military — any military, anywhere. Just as in prehistoric times. Those of you who have been in the armed services will know exactly what I mean. My own service was in the Marines, where nothing less than 110% bureaucracy was tolerated.

I mention this not in any critical way, but merely to offer a perfect example of bureaucratic methods. I am not at all implying that there is something *wrong* with military bureaucracy. On the contrary, I have argued all along that bureaucracy is a method, neither good nor bad in itself, suitable for some tasks and not for others. Obviously we need an army, and obviously an army has to be organized on bureaucratic principles. There is no way to make it a free market proposition. We cannot peddle national defense door to door.

What I find interesting here, and not obvious at all, is how widely specific military forms pervade all areas of the bureaucracy. That is, military methods are the model for key features of *all* bureaucracy. The most innocuous federal office can, on close inspection, be seen to have certain decidedly militaristic qualities. Only in recent years has this been at all apparent in gray flannel Washington, which now boasts at least four full-time military bands ready to strut about on ceremonial occasions. In Old World bureaucracy, however, full-dress military trappings were often *de rigueur,* and the sight of a ranking bureaucrat in a business suit rather than military uniform would have been a surprise.

I would not have guessed much of this, if any of it, before I undertook this little study. It is a strain indeed to suppose that in the breast of a postal clerk there beats the heart of a warrior. Yet there are connections that go back millenia, and clearly enough, even our uniformed postal clerk enjoys many privileges only by virtue of his employment in a coercive State monopoly.

Nock remarked, "The positive testimony of history is that the State invariably had its origin in conquest and confiscation. No primitive State known to history originated in any other manner. . . . Moreover, the sole invariable characteristic of the State is the economic exploitation of one class by another." Given this perspective, it is less taxing to see the ways of the conqueror incorporated into the State organization. Rather, one wonders how the State could possibly be organized except with the ancient military methods. The State, like its military arm, is a command structure, which suggests that forms of military command must be applied to the farthest reaches of the State's bureaucracy.

For instance, all bureaus use some variation of the military chain of command. This is the ultimate expression of the caste system. Everybody in the military, from the lowliest recruit to the commander-in-chief, has a precise rank. Everyone is in place, and everyone knows his place. Between any two points in the organization, the higher rank commands, the lower rank obeys. This is a necessity in the military today even as it was a necessity in the beginning. The first rule for the buck private is to obey; he cannot be allowed to do as he pleases. No more could the nomad commander allow Ugvark over there to do as he pleased, despite his skills at hand-to-hand combat and his eighteen ponies. Command is command. The military action must be focused, organized, unified, unquestionable. Responsibility cannot be divided. Absolute lines of authority and responsibility must be maintained.

So, too, in civilian bureaus. The bureau itself is but a functionary of the State, and cannot be allowed to do as it pleases. Again, authority is absolute, and responsibility cannot be divided. That is the way things have to be in a *legal* system, of which the bureau is part. The bureau must be made responsible to higher authority, and it is. Structurally, it must have a chain of command which, in turn, is incorporated into the larger command structure of the State itself. The bureaucratic chain of command may not be expressed in the harsh terms of the military, but it is similar in every way. A bureau does not have jobs so much as it has *slots*.

Civilian bureaus have also been obliged to borrow the ancient military tie-breaker in case of equal rank, namely, seniority. If authority rests on rank, rank rests on time served. In case of a tie, the trooper with more time in grade is ranking and in absolute command, even if he is only one hour "ahead" after twenty-five years. Such a rule is necessary because there has to be some method of assigning rank that is both instantly clear and indisputable to every bonehead in the service. It is a serious matter, and for good or ill, many a battlefield decision has been settled by the fact that one officer or the other was commissioned a week earlier.

Why isn't command given to the better officer? Because there is no objective measure of merit in the military, just as there is none anywhere in the bureaucracy. There simply is no way to measure military skill or merit in an indisputable way. (This is at heart an economic question, and we see it again and again in the comparison of economic vs. political — bureaucratic — actions. Economic actions can be objectively valued, and bureaucratic actions cannot. This accounts for most if not all of the relative success of economic actions and the relative failures and blunders of bureaucracy.) Why doesn't command flow to the more skillful people in a bureaucracy? Because there is no possible way to judge their skills beyond dispute. Thus the ancient way must apply, and bureaucratic manning tables and pay scales are awash in seniority rules. Merit cannot be determined, but time in grade can, however perverse the result.[1]

Making longevity a factor of command has a curious effect in the military, and as much in civilian bureaus. With seniority rules in effect, the safest, and hence best, way to advance is simply to outlast your competitors. To get ahead, the bureaucrat need do little more than keep his nose clean, wait, and not make waves. The better he can suppress any hint of his own personality, the more likely that his competitors will tire of the game first and move along to something more interesting. Be quiet, be unresourceful, and if you keep at it long enough, you will have a glowing career in the bureaucracy. By this mechanism, rank and authority gradually flow into the hands of the fuddy-duddies. Thus, we often see the least innovative, most rulebook-minded people in charge of the bureau, or effectively in charge even if not in the top slot. And as often as not they are older folks who, after long years in subordinate positions, have lost all initiative and vigor. Should this bureau (or this army) come up against a new or different problem, you can bet the rent that it will find the wrong answer.

The lack of measurable merit has another striking effect in bureaucratic affairs. Namely, it makes politics and personality the key criteria for advancement. If you cannot prove your merit (as you can in business), you have to curry favor with your superior to get ahead. It's that simple. No other arrangement works, for want of objective standards. True, you may get a bit of credit for various tours of duty, or the training courses you take, or the proficiency test you pass. But none of these really

---

[1]A pay scale based on seniority is a dead giveaway that individuals are not being paid according to their productivity, and almost always means the scale is higher than market rates. This is of course true in the bureaucracy itself, and is also common in bureaucratic protectorates among private businesses, notably in labor unions and in "regulated" — i.e., protected — industries. Public education at all levels uses seniority-based pay scales.

measures output, and such standards are all but useless in predicting how a given individual will perform in combat conditions. Therefore, personality takes the place of standards, and politicking is the road to promotion.[2]

There are of course many ways to curry favor with one's superiors, all of which have colorful names in military jargon. One of the rare printable ones is "water walking," which means playing the hotshot. Various forms of backstabbing — undercutting your competitors — are ever popular. The perennial favorite is simple toadying, even if it leaves one with calluses on knees and forehead. If you can pull the right strings or make the right noises, you may be on the fast track for advancement. But it's a cutthroat game, and you may be ambushed by competitors pulling strings of their own. Whatever your style of politicking, success ultimately depends on your superior's judgment of your personality. This is ever risky. If you make waves without making the right impression on higher-ups, you will probably find your career slammed into reverse gear.

Politicking is equally pervasive in civilian bureaucracy, although usually in softer forms. I suspect it accounts for certain of the splashy or bizarre behavior for which bureaucracy is famed. Somewhere along the line, an underling is doing something extreme to catch his superior's attention. Persecute some business to the

---

[2]This points up a seeming paradox. Business managers are given a wide discretion in their actions, yet cannot exercise this authority arbitrarily; the results of what they do will be judged objectively in what Mises calls the "unbribeable tribunal" of profit and loss. Under bureaucracy, in contrast, leaders are part of a chain of command and can be given only the most limited discretion. Yet their actions and advancements are determined in large part by wholly arbitrary judgments of personality. The explanation is this. Business is controlled in its actions by the necessity of serving its customers' wishes. Bureaucrats do not have to please customers and there are no market checks on their behavior. The only restraints on bureaucracy are political.

outer limits of the rulebook, and you may be in line to move up a grade or two. This is hardly an incentive for reasonable behavior, but it is built into any system that operates on personality rather than performance.

If I seem to be making much of the measuring of success, it's because the contrast with private alternatives is so striking and instructive. Business, with its tools of economic calculation, *can* measure success, and with great accuracy. It has, indeed, a variety of informative measures, like productivity, sales, growth, and most importantly, profit and loss. With these tools, business can adjust pay to performance, and promote according to merit. And as a rule, it must do just that, due to the constraints of competition.

Since no such tools are available to bureaucracy, military or civilian, wholly different methods must be used to assign responsibility and duties. Moreover, these methods must satisfy the categorical equalities of legal rules, yet provide concrete, indisputable, and readily recognized guidelines for everybody in the organization. Experience from the earliest times showed the only feasible methods were those of a command structure based on rank, with rank in turn mainly based on seniority. These factors are incorporated in the tortuous pay scales so beloved of governments and their fiefs. Adjustments anywhere in the system are a power game, based on personality and politics. One other standard used for assigning responsibility is size of command, and it is a flawless incentive toward bureaucratic growth. If you were paid or promoted according to how many warm bodies you had in your bureau, wouldn't you use every excuse to add more warm bodies?

Such were the methods devised, of necessity, by the nomad raiders of old to organize their military operations. In every case they remain central to the operation of bureaucracy today, civilian as well as military. Our postal clerk may not be much of a warrior, but he works for a military organization. Infringe on its "territory" — its monopoly on first-class mail — and your actions will be suppressed, if need be by force of arms.

The military must have had the honor of creating the Rulebook Itself for bureaucracy. No physical proof of this has been recovered, so far as I know, but the presumptive case is strong. In any case, the by-the-rules approach still reaches its pinnacle in the military structure and the military mind. I can just hear some drill sergeant for the Hamites or Manchus or Magyars or Scythians or the Hyksos hordes telling recruits, "There are three ways of doing things. The right way, the wrong way, and the Army way."

The rulebook, we have seen, is fundamental to all forms of bureaucracy. It is the law for those who administer the law. Without the rulebook, the law itself would degenerate and lose its force. Government would become wholly arbitrary — and deadly.

* * *

I must stress again at this point that this discussion of the military forms of bureaucracy is in no sense critical. Things are as they are. Not only are bureaucratic methods suitable for both military and civilian agencies, they are the only methods that can work. It would be utterly useless to find fault or complaint in this fact.

Having said as much, however, I must repeat the clear warning of history. The military form of bureaucracy tells exactly what will be our fate unless we bring the bureaucratic structure under control. And all efforts to do so, in the American experience over the past half century, have been conspicuously absent, unavailing or futile. Unless we bring bureaucracy into check, our fate will be military dictatorship, decay, collapse, and ruin. Nowhere in history is there a single exception to this pattern.

This very prospect has been addressed, from differing viewpoints, in two of the most sobering literary works of our times, Orwell's *1984* and Huxley's *Brave New World*. Less known but even more frightening is *That Hideous Strength* by C. S. Lewis,[3] which contemplated life under a "scientific" bureaucracy.

The danger is inherent in all bureaucracy, but is most visible in its military forms. From its beginnings bureaucracy has been a system of coercive exploitation. Even if we find nothing evil in this, the system is parasitic and antiproductive. It produces nothing itself, and its members harm all efforts by others to produce. Bureaucracy therefore shrinks the supply of food and other goods we need for human survival. The more it grows, the more precarious our fate. The greatest danger lies in letting this military marauder spread its tentacles ever further over the economic and private mechanisms our survival depends on. Somehow we have allowed ourselves to believe that intervention by a military organization can "regulate" business or determine wage rates or perform a thousand other social tasks. It cannot. Unless we rid ourselves of this notion, utterly, it will seal our doom.

To look at it from another angle, the military is a slave system. The thought is unpleasant to our modern ears, but that is the fact. Everybody in the military bureaucracy, with the qualified exception of the supreme commander, is a slave. Its mission is, as it has been since genesis of statehood, the control of slaves, or "subjects."

---

[3]The third book of the so-called Space Trilogy. The others are *Out of the Silent Planet* and *Perelandra*. Both of these have fascinating discussions of moral questions, but otherwise do not touch on the subject of bureaucracy.

Its only tool is to give orders backed by the force of arms. If a subject fails to comply, it will punish, jail, or even kill him. If anybody in the organization fails to obey, he too will be dealt with. Dissent and discord cannot be tolerated any more than authority can be divided. While standards may be somewhat relaxed in peacetime, compliance, backed by naked force, becomes absolute in times of war or "emergency," circumstances which are controlled and easily manipulated by the supreme commander. But consider: the bureaucracy is *perpetually* at war with its subject population. It conducts its incursions into private or economic affairs much in the manner of military invasions. It is notorious for its hostility to business; in fact this is "hostility" in the military sense. Not only is the bureaucracy military in form, but military in its attitudes.

In these matters our modern understandings greatly deceive us. Any politician with savvy knows he is engaged in exploitation, in a form of warfare against the people. He may have been attracted to politics in the first place by the tenderhorn notion of doing something for the people or cleaning up the mess in Washington. But if he stays awhile, he learns the ways of power, and knows which side of the struggle he is on. Yet we the people never seem to learn the nature of the game, and turn ever to the State as our friend and protector, a delusion the politicians take endless pains to nourish. In earlier times it was different. You knew where you stood. Either you were extracting "tribute" from a subject population at spearpoint, or you were the one at the wrong end of the spear surrendering your goods or labor. There could be no such misunderstanding as there is now.

In an earlier America, there was no confusion. Our forebears had a very healthy distrust of the State. They had fought for their freedom against a bureaucratic State, and wanted nothing to do with another. It was this attitude, far more than the chains of the Constitution, that limited American government to reasonable bounds. But this attitude finally perished in the traumatic events of the Great Depression and the New Deal days.

Albert Jay Nock had occasion to reflect on this seachange even as it was occurring, in 1935. To Nock, it was evidence even then that America was rejecting its Jeffersonian heritage in favor of statism. And he saw only too well where it would lead:

> Our pride resents the thought that the great highways of New England will one day lie deep under layers of encroaching vegetation, as the more substantial Roman roads of Old England have lain for generations; and that only a group of heavily overgrown hillocks will be left to attract the archaeologist's eye to the hidden debris of our collapsed skyscrapers. Yet it is to just this, we know, that our civilization will come; and we know it because we know that there never has been, never is, and never will be, any disorder in nature — because we know that things and actions are what they are, and the consequences of them will be what they will be.
>
> But there is no need to dwell so lugubriously upon the probable circumstances of a future so far distant. What we and our more nearly immediate descendants shall see is a steady progress in collectivism running off into a military despotism of a severe type. Closer centralization; a steadily growing bureaucracy; State power and faith in State power increasing, social power and faith in social power diminishing; the State absorbing a continually larger proportion of the national income; production languishing, the State in consequence taking over one "essential industry" after another, managing them with ever-increasing corruption, inefficiency and prodigality, and finally resorting to a system of forced labour. Then at some point in this progress, a collision of State interests [i.e., war; this was written four years before the outbreak of WW II], at least as general and violent as that which occurred in 1914, will result in an industrial and financial dislocation too severe for the asthenic social structure to bear; and from this the State will be left to "the rusty death of machinery," and the casual anonymous forces of dissolution will be supreme.

Although Nock died only ten years later, he lived long enough to see himself vindicated on every single point save the last. Needless to say, he was not surprised, although he found no comfort in successful prediction. Only those were surprised who predicted that a new golden age would emerge from the New Deal and the rise of statism in America. In fact, the New Deal was but an American version of the centralist experiments occurring everywhere in those days, most notably in Italy, Germany, and Russia.

The war-end collapse was great but not final. In the victorious allied powers, the cycle Nock predicted started up again, toward an uncertain end. The next violent "collision of State interests," if it occurs, will be rendered infinitely more dangerous by the superpowers' vast arsenals of nuclear weapons. While we as yet have not reached the final chapter, the warning could not be more compelling. We cannot break this ancient cycle until we recognize the nature of bureaucracy and bring it to heel. That is the issue before us. Nock said he was glad he would not live to see how it turned out.

VI

HOW ECONOMIC LAW ORDAINS BUREAUCRATIC FAILURE

> There are [only] two methods for the conduct of affairs within the frame of human society, *i.e.*, peaceful cooperation among men. One is bureaucratic management, the other is profit management.
>
> — Ludwig von Mises

> [Competitive markets are] the only means so far discovered of enabling individuals to coordinate their economic activities without coercion.
>
> — Milton Friedman

> There are two methods, or means, and only two, whereby man's needs and desires can be satisfied. One is the production and exchange of wealth; this is the *economic means*. The other is the uncompensated confiscation of wealth produced by others; this is the *political means* . . . . The State . . . *is the organization of the political means.* (Original emphasis)
>
> — Albert Jay Nock

Economic law is the curse of the ruling class. It keeps getting in the way of the great and well-intended designs of great and benevolent rulers, and making them look a good deal less than omnipotent. And if a ruler can't be all-powerful, what can he be? Omnipotence is not only the right but the duty of every State. Precisely this fact has been vouchsafed us from earliest times by tribal chieftains, warlords, lords, kings, emperors, dictators, presidents, and party bosses, often in a most forceful way. Moreover, the large majority of them, if not in fact all, were and are living gods, so they also vouchsafed us, and if gods are not all-powerful, who is?

An interesting question, don't you think? Why is it that the most powerful and godlike ruler ultimately cannot control the economic behavior of his most loyal and adoring subjects? Why is he not supreme? And if he is not, who — or what — does rule?

The question is not rigged. Somehow, State ventures into economic matters have always come to grief in one way or another. Countless are the monarchs who have tried to dictate economic rules, often with the most fearsome penalties for offenders, only to have their plans laid waste. Roman emperors tried it over and again. Diocletian brought Rome to its knees trying. The French revolutionaries tried it, with all their science, in the springtime of the Enlightenment, and got Napoleon for their trouble. During the Revolutionary War, the Continental Congress flirted with decreeing the death penalty for anyone who would not accept the lawful money it was issuing.[1] Bismarck's subservient universities seriously tried to stamp out the teaching of economics, lest economics detract from the power of the Iron Chancellor. The Soviet Union still shoots people for "economic" crimes, that is, profiting from private enterprise.[2]

---

[1]Called Continental dollars, from which we still have the expression, "Not worth a Continental."

[2]An illustrative example: In the early 1960s, the director and manager of the restaurant at a railroad station in Sverdlovsk invented a new and better machine to fry meats and pies. The machine saved approximately a tenth on an ounce of cooking oil per serving. This added up to about 400 rubles

The question is not whether but why all this occurs. The answer, as I have already intimated, is: economic law. That, plus the surprising fact that, in economic disputes, the power of the State is puny compared to the power of the people. One might as well ask why IBM, or AT&T, or the Postal Service for that matter, cannot repeal the laws of supply and demand. Or why, to recall a well-known case, a state legislature cannot successfully pass a law decreeing that the value of π shall equal 3. It just doesn't work that way. Economics does not always work the way rulers want it to either, but millenia of experience have not yet beaten it into their thick heads. States go right on trying to be omnipotent when it is not possible.

Economics can be both very simple and impossibly abstruse. I prefer the former version. All that it really says, in essence, is that, given any choice, people will act to improve their own well-being, each according to his own unique values, with the least possible effort. Or to put it another way, we all try to get the most we can from life with the least exertion, according to what each of us thinks is most important. How can anyone argue with that? Not only is it self-evidently true, but the supporting evidence is staggering. If we can't take this as a fundamental rule of human behavior, we can't believe anything. Yet it is precisely this quality in us, in all of us, that dooms State meddling with economic matters and makes the bureaucrat an ogre.

Notice two things. This fundamental principle describes human behavior, but does not touch on *economic* behavior; that will follow. Second, note that it puts a profit motive, of sorts, at the root of human action:

---

worth of cooking oil saved per month, which the men pocketed. They were arrested by the KGB, tried, convicted, and, in February, 1963, shot. Death to innovators and profiteers!

we all want to get the most we can out of life. It is hardly a coincidence that this carries over as the dominant feature of our exchanges, our dealings with one another in economic terms. Both parties to any exchange will seek by it to maximize their gain and minimize their cost, as they see it. If they cannot do this, each to his own satisfaction, the exchange will abort; one or both will refuse. This is fundamental too.

We acknowledge, but need not discuss here, the non-economic applications of this principle: the man who renounces worldly goods for spiritual betterment, or the man who drowns plunging into a river to save a child's life, seeks profit in his life, according to his values, as certainly as others pursue great wealth in the market-place. For our purposes, we need only consider economic exchanges, our bread-and-butter dealings with one another.

The profit principle (I will call it) is at the heart of economic law. And economic law will persist as long as people are people. It rests on three indisputable axioms: our individuality (a genetic certainty), hence our unique values and priorities as individuals; our desire for self-betterment (a true universal among living things, and a necessity for survival); and our effort to economize, to maximize our values at least cost (again, a biological imperative for survival). If these three things are true, and most assuredly they are, the laws of supply and demand must follow, along with other basic economic laws.

All supply-and-demand says is that the more a thing costs us, the less we want it, and conversely. This is a flawless echo of the profit principle. In economics it is generally applied to groups or aggregates of people, but no less valid on that account. Keep in mind that the "cost" of a thing may not be dollars; it may be labor or some other item of exchange, or even exasperation.

Having said all this, let us return to the question of why the sovereign, and his bureaucracy, cannot rule economic matters. We have already observed, in detail, that the bureau is a purely political body, a legal body, a part of the State. Let us now consider, briefly, the problems that confront, say, the Central Economic Planning Bureau of the People's Republic of Rapinia. As you recall, Rapinia was long since incorporated into the Soviet Union, and would be all but forgotten today except for its remarkable ethnic purity — and the fact that, as a result, all Rapinians, like one big family, have the best of intentions toward one another. It is the one native trait that the Soviets, despite every effort, have not been able to eradicate. Actually, there's no place on earth quite like it. Rapinians not only wish each other well, but think nothing but the best of their Soviet masters. They have, in fact, like no other Soviet satellite, adopted the socialist system with great enthusiasm, and as usual (in their case) the best of intentions. They are by no means stupid (have you ever heard any Rapinian jokes?), nor backward, and have extensive access not only to Western opinion but to Western technology (most of this admittedly supplied by the KGB). However, their trade with the West is minimal.

The assignment at present facing the CEPB of the PPR of the USSR is this: "Improve Rapinia's economic situation — or else. Cordially, /s/ M. Gorbachev."

How shall this be done? Ponder the problems. The Central Economic Planning Bureau must organize countless millions of production factors — every detail of the tools, raw materials, transportation, power systems, plants, and the Rapinian work force, into a coherent system that maximizes the production of the desired goods and services. This alone, despite the importation of the most advanced ideas and technologies, is a brain-boggling, almost incomprehensible task. But the problems have only begun. What *are* the goods and services desired for the improvement of Rapinia's economic situation? We go back to square one. What, in order of priority, is needed? The Bureau must decide. Only then can it ask, how shall we select the best procedures for *each* of the many goods and services desired? And how, at last, shall we weave together a grand strategy employing the best of the innumerable technologies available to us in every case, to utilize the millions of production factors most efficiently for each of the outputs we must decide on, to achieve maximum success?

This is not hypothetical. It is the problem that faces all the central economic planners in all the socialist paradises, and good intentions will not solve it. It is a problem that would strain the resources of a thousand mainframe computers (Rapinia happens to have four, all of them purchased illicitly).

And the problem is very much worse that I have painted it as yet. Suppose Rapinia had a thousand mainframe computers and plenty of qualified people to program them — what would they feed into the machines? There is nothing to put in. No information exists that can help the planners. The planners have at their disposal reliable statistics about Rapinian production of steel I-beams, shoes, wheat, toothpaste, dental drills, and so on. But what are two kilos of soap powder *worth* relative to a hectare of barley relative to a hydroelectric dam? How can one add up, or make any calculations concerning, an I-beam, wheat, and cosmetics? There is no common denominator for these things, for the complex array of goods and services that makes up the Rapinian economic output. You simply cannot add up I-beams, toothpaste, and shoes, *in kind,* any more that you can average apples and oranges.

The assignment is impossible. Oh, the CEPB will

make decisions and allot so much toothpaste, and so much wheat, and so many galoshes, and so many hydroelectric projects, to the citizenry. Comrade Gorbachev has said that this must be done, and it is done. But the CEPB hasn't a clue whether it was done right. In fact it was not. It can't be.

Resources are, after all, limited. If the CEPB chooses to do one thing, it must forego all other potential uses for those resources. One choice settles things; all other options are thereafter closed, all other opportunities lost. Given literally infinite possibilities, there's no chance the planning board will stumble on the best plan, or even anything close. Your odds for solving a scrambled Rubik's cube by closing your eyes and twirling it a few dozen times (one in forty-three quintillion) look attractive in comparison.

Things get even worse. Economic conditions in Rapinia change even as the CEPB is trying to grapple with them. In fact, each decision by the Bureau changes the situation. The cost of the factors of production in the projects it favors goes up; those in other projects go down. The Bureau, having studied economics in the West, knows this, but cannot detect it, much less measure it, when it occurs right under their noses.

And worse yet. Rapinians, for all their good intentions, go right on acting as all humans do, according to their individual values and the profit principle. When the decisions of CEPB fail to motivate them properly, or reward them adequately for their efforts, or limit their work burden, or make available to them the things they want, the Rapinians adjust their lives and actions to get along the best they can. This, of course, occurs constantly. The Bureau has no possible way to take individuals' needs and values and skills into account, nor any way to adjust its programs to individuals. Individual performance therefore falls disappointingly short of what might be expected from good little social units. Comrade Gorbachev calls this sabotage, even though Rapinian workers have been extremely conscientious in trying to make the plan succeed.

What happens to Rapinia as the plan proceeds, you can well imagine, without the benefit of economic theory. It shares the real-life fate of all the socialist countries. The plan simply interferes with the existing economy and makes matters worse. However weak the economy may have been, it had at least gone through enough adjustment and human arrangements to produce something. The plan scraps all this in favor of blueprint notions that have no relation to reality; the harder the Bureau pushes, the more damage it does. Life in Rapinia is reduced to a bare subsistence level for all but the Party bosses. Somehow, the country manages to overfulfill its quota for arms production, but consumer goods, even food, become very scarce. People have to get up at dawn to stand in line for food, and the endless hours they waste doing so are a dead loss to productivity. A once cheerful people become gray, grim, and worn.

As we take our leave from a desperate Rapinia, do you see what is amiss in this whole scheme of central planning? What is missing?

The answer, simply stated, is *economic information.* The Central Economic Planning Bureau has nothing to work with except coercion. It does not have and cannot employ what Mises calls the tools of economic calculation.

All *economic* information is derived from free markets. But Rapinia has no free markets. The State, of course, owns all the means of production, and dictates the prices of goods and services and wages. The Bureau cannot get an inkling of the true state of economic affairs, and never will under this system. It is perfectly helpless to undertake economic management. Its only recourse is an unbelievably crude political management that can barely keep people alive — if that.

In contrast, open markets in America and the Western world provide economic information in profusion. At the heart of it are the ever-fluctuating market prices of all goods, services, and capital. *Market price is the common denominator that is missing in Rapinia.* It is market price, and this alone, that lets us compare that steel I-beam to wheat to galoshes, and so on. It is market price alone that lets us judge the success of any enterprise, according to its relative profit or loss. It is market price that enables us to calculate the prospects for the success of a new enterprise, and steers us away from those that will fail and waste scarce resources. It is market price that tells us when and what to buy or not to buy; which resources are abundant and which scarce; when to use a resource freely and when to conserve it (oil, for instance). It is market price that best enables us to use the profit principle to advantage in our own lives — that tells us how we can maximize our satisfactions in life, whatever our unique goals happen to be, at the least cost. Without the economic information from free market prices, the modern world could not exist and progress would be impossible.

All *economic* calculation and planning is based on market prices (as opposed to political planning by State bureaus). And market prices can only emerge from free and open markets in which all participate, according to their individual values and resources. Markets can be free only if the means of production are privately owned, and if full freedom of exchange exists. Where the State owns the means of production, dictates prices and wage rates, and suppresses the freedom of exchange, no economic information is available and economic calculation is out of the question. Under socialism, economic planning is impossible.

This, in bare outline, is the crushing refutation of bureaucratic management advanced sixty years ago by Professor Ludwig von Mises, the greatest of the Austrian school of market economists. There is no reply to it. Russians were far better dressed and fed in 1910 than they are today after sixty-five years of relentless Soviet efforts to make socialism work. It can't be done.

As Mises put it, trying to manage economic matters without the tools for it is like being blind and deaf:

> It is true that under socialism there would be neither discernible profits nor discernible losses. Where there is no calculation, there is no means of getting an answer to the question whether the projects planned or carried out were those best fitted to satisfy the most urgent needs; success and failure remain unrecognized in the dark. The advocates of socialism are badly mistaken in considering the absence of discernible profit and loss an excellent point. It is, on the contrary, the essential vice of any socialist management. It is not an advantage to be ignorant of whether or not what one is doing is a suitable means of attaining the ends sought. A socialist management would be like a man forced to spend his life blindfolded.

The full significance of the nonmarket, political character of bureaucracy should now become clear. Devoid of any economic information or mechanisms, the bureau can never develop the tools for economic calculation and planning. It is helpless and manifestly unfit to manage economic enterprises of any sort. It will harm anything it touches. If it is charged with directing or regulating the entire economy, it will ruin the economy. Moreover, the harm it does is progressive; the greater the reach of bureaucracy, the more the damage multiplies —and this will inevitably be the excuse for more totalitarian measures. None of this can be avoided any more than economic law itself.

The implications of Mises' critique go even further.

They mark socialism not only as hopelessly inferior to, but *dependent* upon free markets in other countries. On this shoal all dreams of world socialism founder and die.

Even now, the socialist bloc depends heavily on economic information from free Western markets, especially ours.[3] The information socialist planners get from Western markets is slow, and does not reflect local markets; but what else can they use? In their own "markets," the means of production are State-owned and prices are dictated. No useful information can be derived from them.

Were the Soviets to conquer the world for socialism, where would they get the information needed for economic calculation? They would be reduced to the hopeless problem of comparing steel I-beams to galoshes in kind, with no common denominator. And their system would collapse and shatter into a million pieces. Armed force cannot hold the world together. Insofar as the Soviets are aware of this, and there is reason to think they are, they must have decidedly mixed emotions about the progressive bureaucratization of Western markets. If our markets go, there goes their source of information.

In fact, socialist planners have long been aware of Mises' critique. No less a figure in the Soviet revolution than Leon Trotsky conceded its validity. Lenin had to abandon pure socialist economics after a few years, and reintroduce a degree of freedom and private ownership, to keep the country from starving to death. Despite these bitter lessons in reality, Soviet planners go right on trying to find a socialist substitute for economic planning. All their attempts have failed, of course, and will always fail. There is none.

---

[3]In the Comecon, the Soviet bloc's version of the European Common Market, the national currencies of the various socialist member nations are pegged against the U.S. dollar.

There will never be a way to determine accurately the relative values of goods, services, and capital except through the workings of free markets. The reason is fundamental. Only the free market can represent the evaluations of all people in their constantly changing needs and capacities. The socialist "alternative"represents the ignorant opinion of a few, imposed by political force on all.

Value is subjective — a matter of opinion. There is no absolute or *objective* measure of value.[4] There is no measure a planner can turn to that says, for instance, that every adult needs six grams of soap powder a day. Things just don't work that way. In real life, one person may want five grams, another ten, three others want bar soap, two liquid soap, and that unpleasant fellow at the edge of town doesn't use any. In a word, as unique individuals, we value different things differently, and our priorities change all the time. I may be eager to buy a new shirt today, but change my mind tomorrow.

It is because people value things differently that there is such a thing as a market, or a horse race. Every exchange we make represents a difference of value-opinion. If I buy that shirt, it is because in this case I value the money I spend less than the shirt, whereas the merchant values the money more than the shirt. Without this difference in values, there would be no exchanges. And suppose, before I get to the store, a stack of bills comes in, and I decide I can't afford the shirt after

---

[4]Marx, in his labor theory of surplus value, postulated that value was in fact absolute and objective, and that all economic output could be explained by present and past labor. From this he deducted that all profits are theft, and that all capitalists are, well, pigs. His theory managed to overlook motivation, decisions, capital, management, skill, luck, and discovery, among other things. It is so simple-minded, shoddy, and badly reasoned that it disappeared from economic thought around 1870 — except in the socialist countries.

all. My values have shifted overnight; now I need the money more than the shirt. If all people were identical and consumed exactly the same things in the same amounts, if we were all perfect little social units, then and only then would socialist planning be possible. Of course we are not alike and never will be; that is genetically certain.

Moreover, value, in the market sense, is a much stronger and firmer measure than the sort of opinion one dashes off for, say, a Gallup Poll. Talk is cheap. For instance, there is a poll around showing that most people are in favor of compulsory air bags for cars. It would, they say, make driving safer and save lives. Talk is indeed cheap. When General Motors offered the air bags as an option, nobody bought them. GM had to discontinue the air bags. When it came to a choice of having to pay extra money for the air bag, nobody wanted to pay the price. That is the kind of opinion you can count on. That is market value. It is value so deeply felt that it moves people to act: to buy or not to buy; to invest or not to invest. The market incorporates all such real opinion.[5]

And more: as unique individuals, each of us knows his own values better, by far, than anybody else can. Nobody else can really speak for what we are, what we need, what we desire. It is the work of a lifetime even to understand one's own spouse with any acuity, and even this does not approach self-knowledge. How can a

---

[5]It is worth noting that politicians, when they are out to skin you with a new program, invariably cite the cheap-talk sort of opinion. They will use polls showing that people want this or the other thing, or they need that and that. It's all hot air. If people want something, they buy it, and if they don't want it, they don't buy it. *That* is the kind of opinion you can count on. When you hear a politician promising to do wonderful things for you, you can bet your shirt that you're about to get soaked. The only legitimate thing a politician can do for you is get off your back.

bureaucratic planner who has never met you make any intelligent economic decisions on your behalf? It cannot be done. Instead of planning for you, the planner must treat you as an interchangeable unit. A faceless unit is all you can be under socialism. Your purpose is to fill a bureaucratic slot.

The market, in complete contrast, represents all of us as we really are, according to our actual decisions and resources. With every dollar we earn or spend, we all give our true values to the marketplace. Every penny is a vote in this economic democracy, and every vote is counted. Our willingness or refusal to enter the market every hour of every day directs and manages all economic production and activity. The information flowing in and out of markets does not stop at national borders, but is linked worldwide in a huge, interdependent world community. No decision made or action taken is without its effect throughout the system. The system reflects us all, to the exact extent that each of us wishes. It even keeps the Soviets from collapsing. Yet, for all its far-reaching effects and complexity, there is nothing at all mysterious about the market. It is the sum of free exchanges — people everywhere acting in an economic capacity, and interacting with one another.

The choice Mises put before us is this: do we determine value by the political process, in which a relative handful of planners make economic decisions for all, and impose them by force (bureaucratic method); or will values be determined by everyone in the marketplace, with each person speaking from self-knowledge about his personal desires and means (profit management)? This is not so much a choice between the few and the many as between the grossly ignorant, slow, and biased opinion of the few as against the self-knowledge of the many. The values dictated by a central planning bureau are unspeakably crude and primitive compared to the market. Even if the bureau members had IQs of 1000 and the most angelic intentions, they could not do the job. They could not begin to understand the infinite diversity and unique needs of millions of other people. The thought of it is ludicrous. All the planners can do is substitute their own values for yours, by force. This is, literally, a stone-age method, and numbingly crude compared to the infinitely more sophisticated, accurate, and representative economic information of the marketplace.

In rational terms, this is no contest. If we choose reason, we choose the market. Unfortunately, that is not the question as between the bureaucratic and profit methods. The dispute is over plunder. Bureaucratic planning is simply an extension of the ancient nomads' control over their subjects, for purposes of exploitation. It is in my opinion wholly incompatible with human dignity and freedom. It crushes individuality and humane values and creativity. The market system would be superior if it were no more than a vehicle for our economic well-being: the prosperity of the West vs. the poverty of the East. But what attracts me to it, and I'm sure others as well, is precisely that the market system reflects and enhances moral values. It is the open market, not a central bureaucracy, that reflects and respects the individual; that allows diversity, dissent, pluralism, a free press, privacy, spiritual expression, and so many other things we hold dear. None of this can be tolerated under Kremlin-style central dictation.

* * *

I agree with Mises that the case against bureaucracy is at this point not only decisive but overwhelming. But it may be that some of you are not yet convinced; and perhaps others, who are, would like more ammunition.

As it happens, there are at least two other top trump cards that the market holds over bureaucracy. Again, in both cases, the bureaucracy runs afoul of nothing less than economic law, with fatal results. I'll discuss both briefly.

The first concerns profit and loss. According to Marx, and Marxism, profits are theft. And needless to say, no government bureau is, or should be, run for a profit. A bureau generally does not charge for its services, and it certainly does not depend on the patronage of satisfied customers for its revenues. A bureau could not act disinterestedly, or in the public interest, so the argument runs, if it were out grubbing for profits. Let's assume that this is so. Yet its detachment from the profit system is a terrible weakness of bureaucracy. Profits are not merely earnings but the market yardstick of efficiency: of success or failure. Bureaucracy, cut off from all economic measurement, has no comparable mechanism to judge whether its own efforts are worthwhile or useless. It has no standard to evaluate its own performance. Here again we find bureaucracy utterly blind about what it is doing or trying to do. To appreciate this, put yourself in the bureaucrat's position and imagine devoting your life's energy to this project or that without ever knowing whether you're doing anybody any good. In business, you can't even afford such reflections. Either you do some good, in a measurable way, or you're out.

Now compare this inherent blindness to the measuring role profits play in economic calculation. In the free market, consumers rule. You, in your production capacity, must serve. Demand is the employer, supply is the employee. What people want and are willing to pay for (demand) determines what will be produced, when, in what quantity, and with what quality. This demand is what you must serve in the market, whatever you are selling —your corn, your brains, your labor. If you don't serve others, as *they* want it, you don't get paid.

But you don't do this willy-nilly. The profit system is equally useful to you in that it allows economic calculation. You are never forced to sell your corn, or brains, or labor at an unsatisfactory rate. Profit lets you calculate what *is* acceptable to you. If you don't profit, you don't sell. The same reasoning is at the heart of the most enormous and complicated business ventures.

Like the bureaucratic planner, the entrepreneur must weigh the myriad factors of production. Millions of them. But unlike the planner, he has the tools to do it. Market prices allow him to compare costs and assess the various strategies he might employ. And potential profitability gives him a yardstick to judge success or failure. Only if a proposed project appears to be profitable, if its potential returns exceed its costs, can he consider it. And then only if the prospective profit compares favorably with other possible projects, other uses for his capital, will he proceed. In this process the businessman, seeking the most efficient use of resources, offers the greatest economic benefit to his consumers. Such economic planning, based on market information, almost unwittingly takes into account the full range of potentials and human needs throughout the entire world, linked together in world markets.

But profit is not just a planning tool. It is an instant measure of success in any established venture at any time. In this age of computers, the information is available in a split second. One needs only look at the profit and loss statement to see how things are going. If the operation is profitable, it means that you are meeting the needs of others, as the market demands, and doing it *efficiently*. (If you are not, somebody else will take your profits away.) Opponents of the market system may choke on the fact all they please, but profits signal your success in serving your fellow humans. The greater your profits, the better you are doing. Competitors will see to it that you cannot charge too much for the goods and services you sell. Therefore, only by serving, helping, enriching others can you improve your profits. Everybody who runs a business knows this —and that it isn't easy. If all the intellectuals who find this degrading were obligated to make their living serving others by making a profit in business, I don't think we'd hear much more criticism of businessmen from them.

Profit, considered as a tool of calculation and a yardstick of success or failure, tells us all of these things and more — and the information is indispensable to maintaining a modern economy. We have to have it to provide food, clothing, and shelter to an increasingly populous world. Unfortunately, statists of all types, not least the bureaucrats, do not recognize the role profits really play. Indeed, most of them have a deep, unreasoning prejudice against profits per se, one that traces back to Marx's foolish labor theory of surplus value.

Profit, in their view, is still something bad, "unearned," stolen from workers. This view ignores the contributions made to production by the savings (capital) of the investor, the effort and ingenuity of the entrepreneur, and the decisions of management; but there is no arguing with prejudice.

Under this mindset, profit reflects greed, and "huge" profits are the result of "unconscionable greed." This is nonsense. Any businessman who tries to be greedy instead of serving his customers will soon get a painful lesson in management from his competitors. The statists do not understand that a businessman cannot dictate his profits, especially "huge" ones. He cannot even predict his profits with any certainty. Profits are not in any way fixed in advance; they are not tied to the size of an investment or the time an entrepreneur spends bringing a project to market. Profits result only from serving the wishes of consumers, and doing it efficiently. If a new product or service delights the buying public, the entrepreneur may profit beyond his wildest dreams. And the chance of this, however remote, motivates many. But it is much more common to experience disappointing profit levels or losses. And that brings up the other factor the statists leave out of their thinking: for every "huge" profit, there are thousands of disappointments and failures. The opportunity to succeed in the market necessarily includes the possibility of failing. Let me put it starkly: without failure there is no success. Business failures are not without value: losses are another tool of economic calculation, and a persuasive teacher. Moreover, any measure to protect against economic loss by political means, by bureaucratic decree, necessarily also limits success and opportunity. Profit and risk are opposite sides of the same coin. Let's now look at the risk side.

* * *

Profit is never automatic. Inseparable from the prospect of making profits is the possibility of loss: risk. No economic enterprise is without risk, simply because the future is unknown. People's wishes change. Tastes change. Customers are fickle. The producer never can say for certain that his product will be accepted by consumers. Almost everyone is a producer in this sense, not only the businessman, but the farmer marketing his crops or the worker marketing his labor. We are all at the mercy of the consumers we serve, and are all at risk. Who knows what tomorrow will bring? Consumer preferences may change, and we may be out of business or out of a job. We do the best we can, but there are no guarantees of success. None of us in the marketplace can *force* customers to buy.

Thus the factor of risk enters all economic planning. And in its way, it is as important as any measure of success. You have to know when to quit as well as when to move ahead.

Whatever your employment or business, your time, labor, money, and credit are limited. Lack of adequate profit tells you when you are failing. Money or other losses tell you when you have failed in meeting the needs of consumers. At that point you must either correct the problem or you're out of business. You cannot sustain unlimited losses.

Loss thus draws a sharp, clear line between what works and what doesn't in the workaday world. Loss supplies to economic enterprise an essential discipline that is altogether lacking in bureaucracy. Enterprises that are unproductive, that fail to serve, that have outlived their usefulness, must be swept away without a backward glance. This is the heart of economic regeneration and progress. The discipline of the market serves our collective interests the same way that clearing the deadwood keeps the forest healthy and makes room for new growth. When a business fails or falters, when losses occur, capital flows to the more productive, ingenious, and efficient enterprises that serve people better. This should not be the cause for any lasting regret. After all, history is littered with the bones of companies that once flourished by making bullet molds, antimacassars, buggy whips, stagecoaches, and a million other things past and gone. Should we mourn their passing, or "protect" the workers in those troubled industries? Or should we look ahead to something better?

Without the risk factor, businessmen would have no way to sort out the good from the hopeless. As profit measures success, loss measures failure, and without this yardstick we would still be doing things the way they were done from ancient times. Entrepreneurs must risk their time and money to back their hopes for new ventures. In doing this, they give us far, far more than we realize: they give us a better future.

* * *

Bureaucracy, in contrast, almost literally rules us from the past. Bureaus literally *are* creatures of the past, and it affects everything they do. Even the recent models have origins in laws that are years or decades old, and many bureaus go back a century or more. Their roots go back even further, to the conditions that gave rise to the law. Those conditions have certainly changed by now, or perhaps disappeared. But the bureau is charged to deal with them, its rulebook was devised to deal with them, and deal with them it does. All bureaus are thus doomed to live in a world gone by. Amending the law and changing their rules does not help; the law is far too slow to catch up with the changing real world. Moreover, the law is always reactionary, reacting to and dealing with past events. It never looks forward (except to raise future taxes). Much of our bureaucratic problem today is the handiwork of legislators long dead, dealing with times long gone. It is not for nothing that we speak of bureaucratic action as "the dead hand of government."

Bureaus not only live in the past, they seem to love it. They are notorious for their kicking-and-screaming resistance to anything that even hints of change. Their whole business is to keep things just as they were when their rulebook was written. They never miss a chance to recite their family tree, down to the very line, paragraph, subchapter, chapter, section, and Act of Congress, signed, sealed, and properly dated, that authorized their existence. I scarcely exaggerate: whole forests have been cleared so that bureaus can include this pedigree in the flood of pamphlets and papers they issue. It is this authority that keeps them on the job when, by any normal standards, their actions would be judged ludicrous. Until just a few years ago, for instance, the government maintained a rope factory in New England to rig its sleek and dreaded men o' war — the ships that brought us victory in the War of 1812. Really. It also had, and may still have, a tea-tasting board, in the grand English tradition that provoked the Boston Tea Party and the American Revolution. It has Civil War, Indian War, Spanish-American War laws. It has scads of World War I emergency laws on the books, and World War I advisory boards in operation, just in case that war happens to flare up. You never can tell about these things! Not if you are in government bureaus.

And that is the point. Bureaus live in the past because they have no way to do anything else. They have no tools to look ahead, even if they wanted to, which, as a rule, they do not. Bureaus have no stake in progress. They have no way to promote progress. It seems to me a minor miracle that anybody can reconcile the existence of bureaucracy with the idea of a better future. Only the entrepreneur can give us the innovations that will make tomorrow brighter. This is economic law.

It all goes back to the factor of economic risk. There is, we have seen, no chance of success if there is no possibility of failure. All economic activity is subject to risk, and all therefore depends on measuring success and failure objectively. Loss and profit provide that measure, the stop-and-go lights for every economic action. Bureaucracy has no profit, no loss, and no risk, so it has no yardstick to guide us — or itself — into the future.

Consider: what conceivable risk is there in bureaucracy? Certainly it does not exist at the pleasure of its customers. It has no customers, produces nothing that people would be willing to buy, and need never please the buying public to stay in operation. Unlike any business, bureaucracy *can* force us to buy its services, be they good, bad or wretched, because it is supported by taxes. Our wishes, in other words, have nothing to do with a bureau's operations. The bureau need only please its congressional masters to prosper, and that takes little more effort than making the right noises from time to time.

Nor can a bureau look at its profit-and-loss statement to see how it's doing. It doesn't have one. For this reason, the bureau does not have and never can have an objective measure of its performance. Even if it did have a "P&L" of some sort, it could not show real profits or losses, because the bureau does not perform according to economic criteria. Bureaus don't know what a loss is. They can, and do, lose money more or less forever, and it makes not a bit of difference to them. Somebody else gets stuck with the bill. The only measure bureaus have of their own efforts is political opinion, a standard far too vague and subjective to be of any use in complex human affairs. Relying on political feedback for direction is about effective as relying on your next-door neighbor's opinions to manage IBM.

The bureaucrats themselves experience no risk in their own pockets. They do not, after all, back what they are doing, as entrepreneurs do, with their own money or resources. They never suffer losses. They can scarcely even lose their jobs, except for the most outrageous (read: politically embarrassing) conduct. Bureaucrats fired "for cause" are a negligible number, perhaps a couple of hundred cases a year out of millions in the bureaucratic work force. (More people than that, in an equal-size statistical sample, would go crazy, or commit rape, armed robbery, or murder.) Nowhere, therefore, do bureaucrats experience risk. Since there is no risk to their agency or to themselves, bureaucrats always can (and always do) plead that they could do the job better if only they had more money (your money). It's a cheap excuse, and they couldn't use it if they had to pay for their own mistakes, as everybody in the market does.

Without a risk factor, bureaucracy is stone blind and brakeless. It has no way to tell when to quit. It can't discern when its programs outlive their usefulness, or turn sour; it can't sort out and throw out the deadwood. Nothing comes closer to eternal life in this earth than a bureaucratic program. Somewhere it is written in the bureaucratic stars that, although men live and die, a factory to make rope for 1812 warships shall never die.

Here again we see the stark contrast between profit management and bureaucratic management, between an organization that can objectively assess and regulate its own activity and one that cannot. The logic of this is that bureaucracy, by its nature, is doomed to capricious, futile, and wasteful efforts — and this is exactly what its handiwork is judged to be, by people everywhere.

Bureaucracy runs afoul of yet one more economic law, with results that can only multiply the damage from its blind economic interventions.

* * *

The supply and demand of a given good or service are brought into balance at the market price. For this to occur, prices must be free to move, to fluctuate at all times, to adjust to ever-changing supply and demand factors. Continual adjustments in price thus serve the indispensable function of *clearing the market* — keeping the goods moving, as it were. The point at which supply and demand are in balance and goods are freely exchanged is called the market-clearing price.

Here's how it works. The market is a continuous

auction. If the supply of a good is greater or less than demand (as determined by buy and sell offers), the price falls or rises accordingly, until equilibrium is restored at the market-clearing price. At this price level, no demand is unsatisfied and no supplies are left to rust or rot. (This so even though some *potential* customers and suppliers, hoping for a better price, temporarily stay out of the market.) As new supply and demand information is received from world markets, prices move constantly, facilitating the free flow of goods, labor, and money from those who offer them to those who want them more and hence are willing to pay the market price for them. (If the thought of "paying the market price for money" sounds strange, that is what you are doing by selling goods or labor in exchange for money.)

Without this market-clearing function of free prices, very bad things start to happen. If prices are unable to move freely, either a glut or a shortage of goods will invariably develop, depending on whether the price is too high or too low. (Which means, higher or lower than the price set by the market auction.) The costs of gluts and shortages, of misdirected economic effort, do not appear in any official ledgers or statistics, but they are always present, grow rapidly, and can in a very short time bring down the most powerful nation on earth.

The *only* thing that can keep prices from moving freely is government action: wage-price controls. Such action, by rulers who deem themselves omnipotent, has occurred throughout all of recorded history. Among the very oldest clay tablets, the records of ancient civilizations uncovered by archaeologists, are price-fixing decrees by the government. Apparently the rulers of old, like the rulers today, tried in their benevolence to their subjects to keep wage rates high and consumer prices low, by imperial decree. This cannot possibly work, and it is one of those things that always leaves egg on the face of His

Omnipotent Holiness, the Sovereign. As I noted at the outset, economic law is the curse of the ruling class. Wage-price fixing violates economic law. And people power — in property, money, and economic capacity — expressed in the marketplace, is stronger than any ruler.

We see the truth of this every time the government tries to fix prices or wage rates (which are also prices, for labor), by force. The government obviously does not fix the price at the market level; this serves no purpose. Besides, if it tried, a price frozen correctly in the morning would be too high or too low by afternoon. So the government does not try. Instead, it tries to please either producers, by fixing the price of goods at artificially high levels, or consumers, by setting the price too low (e.g., "to fight inflation"). But in so doing, it cannot succeed in *its own objectives*, no matter how savage its punishment of violators (the death penalty has been tried many times and at least debated in this country). It only succeeds in wrecking the market-clearing function and blocking the flow of goods from producer to user, and the flow of capital from consumer to producer. That's when real trouble sets in.

Suppose the government fixes a given price too high, that is, above what the market would have dictated. Producers will then expand their operations because the fiat "price" is so attractive, and will supply more of the good than customers want. Simultaneously, consumer purchases decline at the higher price. A glut then develops. The government can do one of two things at this point. It can restrict production by force, by rationing production facilities and banning all others, for example, creating acreage allotments for growing tobacco or peanuts. This gives monopoly status to the holders of government allotments, and one can even imagine the possibility of a peanut farmer becoming so wealthy as to be able to run for the presidency of the United States.

The other option is for the government to buy up the surplus, to keep the price propped up. This, of course, it does with your money, so you end up paying higher consumer prices *and* higher taxes, to keep producers producing too much. This is presently the case with U.S. dairy production, grain and sugar, among other things.

In the past, the list has been far longer. Washington recently announced that it was, no doubt benevolently, going to distribute surplus cheese to the poor. But why does it have surplus cheese? Because, in response to intensive lobbying by the dairy industry, it has fixed prices for dairy products at twice the world level: with about $2 billion of your taxes *plus* the doubled price you pay for milk or butter or cheese. Why doesn't it give away more than a tiny fraction of the surplus cheese it is storing in caves? Because that would "depress" the dairy prices, that is, bring them back to normal. This is forbidden by law. What about the government's enormous hoards of powdered milk and butter? Those cannot be sold here either, or distributed to the needy, lest we interfere with dairy farmers' privileges. We cannot, by law, even give the stuff to the needy in Poland. We did sell some butter to New Zealand recently, at less than the world price, on the strict condition that is not be resold in this country. It is, after all, important to keep American consumers paying far too much for dairy products. Isn't it?

Similarly, suppose the government sets wage rates too high. This it has done for "organized" labor for fifty years, through one-sided and government-enforced "bargaining," minimum wages, and other protectionist laws without number. Does all this raise general wages? Of course not. The laws do not create any new wealth with which to pay the workers; they do not increase the wage pool. (Actually, they reduce it.) All that occurs is a redistribution of income. Protected union workers get artificially high wages, at the expense of lower wages or unemployment for the unprotected workers. In other words, the government makes it possible for the protected, high-income workers to steal jobs, income, and bread from the poor, all this, of course, in the name of "justice" for workers. Why, then, doesn't every worker join a union? This, I believe, *is* the main point of the law — to induce workers to organize or join unions, and thereby become wards of government privilege. Subject, of course, to government control. Meanwhile, if everybody joined a union, there would be no wage privilege for doing so, and the whole wage structure should, theoretically, revert to market levels — except that at this point it would all be under the bureaucratic thumb. And that would not create fair wages.

The phenomenon of the overpaid worker (usually grossly overpaid), seems to appear, with no exception that I can find, in every industry "regulated" by bureaucrats; certainly not least in the bureaucracy itself. It started with regulation of the railroads by the Interstate Commerce Commission a century ago, spread to other forms of transportation — barges, trucks, cars, merchant marine, airlines, then spread further to anything that even resembled interstate commerce, such as power generation, communications, and — raising chickens.[6] And it brought every industry so regulated to the brink of bankruptcy. What the bureaucrats and regulators never understand is that the *market* sets wage rates, not government decrees; that the government cannot repeal

---

[6]In a celebrated case some years ago, federal courts ruled that federal legislators could tell a farmer what to do with the chickens in his back yard, with the force of law, because, see, if the chickens weren't in his back yard, they might be in the market, and if they are in the market, they might affect interstate commerce. By such "interpretation," the Constitution, which prohibits federal intervention except for commerce that crosses state lines, has been made to permit federal intervention into your back yard.

the laws of supply and demand. If you raise an industry's costs by imposing artificially high wage rates, the industry has to raise its prices — and demand for its product goes down. Its profits decline. And as it becomes less and less profitable, the industry attracts less investment, pays more for loans, and finally cannot raise new capital at all. Next stop: bankruptcy, unless the government steps in (again), with aid, e.g., Lockheed, Chrysler, Conrail. Which means it must supplement the industry's artificially depressed revenues with higher taxes that you and I must pay. One intervention leads to another, and another: every subsidized company or industry is ripe for even more excessive wage demands, greater dependency for the industry, higher subsidies ...

Damaging as this process is, we face a greater and more immediate threat when government fixes prices too low. This it typically does when it is busy stealing the country's wealth by inflating the money supply. This causes prices to rise to painfully high levels, and causes a lot of grumbling among the victims (consumers). Then, benevolently, the government fixes consumer prices at low levels, to "protect" us, or at least to keep us from grumbling.

The result, almost at once, is shortages. On the one hand, we consumers want more of the goods at their low, fixed prices. On the other hand, suppliers cannot produce or sell the goods profitably — and more and more refuse to do so. The flow of goods to the market dwindles and finally stops. And then there is little or nothing to buy. Starvation is literally threatening at this point, so the government must intervene again, at once, if it has not already done so. Its options are, first, to try to force producers to sell at the low price. This just doesn't work. Even today, in the socialist bloc, farmers can resist having to sell their meat and produce to the State. Insofar as producers can be forced to sell, it is a one-time, short-term solution, limited to stocks on hand; future production cannot be sustained at great loss, and is even more damaged by eating the seed corn and the breeding herds. Second, the government can raise prices (socialist countries), or remove the controls and let prices rise naturally (Western countries). In either case, it is defeating its original objective, and is going to take a lot of heat from angry consumers. Thus it usually turns to its third, and last, option: rationing. Any economy-wide rationing scheme is by its nature miserably wasteful and corrupting and easily avoided by determined consumers. But it has a "noble"-sounding rationale, that everybody is getting his "fair" share of the scarce goods. So it is a great favorite with governments, which, in imposing the rationing scheme, get their sticky fingers into everything.

All of this we have seen in our own country in recent years. President Nixon's wage and price controls in August 1971 soon produced shortages in thousands of items. The controls went through three or four generations or "phases" of increasingly labyrinthine bureaucratic regulations, but, somehow, it was the same old story. Consumers couldn't buy what they wanted and producers wouldn't produce at a loss. The controls were finally scrapped, although several of the bureaus charged with administering them survived. (Same old story!) All price controls were scrapped, that is, except those on the oil industry. The government used a form of rationing, regional fuel allocation and "entitlements" to keep oil prices "low," and we all paid dearly for it. Do you remember waiting hours in lines at gas stations, and then being able to buy only five or ten gallons? But our miseries in gas lines were relatively small. Those long, grim lines of people today in Poland or the other socialist countries, waiting hour after hour in the hope of buying soap or bread or other bare necessities of life, eloquently demonstrate the folly of state intervention in the market to fix prices or wages.

The cost of this folly, in scarce resources and human life, is almost beyond belief. Production facilities are destroyed; capital and seed corn are wastefully consumed. Corruption and privilege are epidemic under rationing. Most hurtful, in my mind, is that the tens of millions of hours Polish shoppers, and other victims of State benevolence, must wait in line every day, are a total waste of human potential. The government-induced glut of guns in the Soviet Union, and butter in this country, are likewise a total waste of scarce resources. All of this occurs because the State has interfered with free prices, and for no other reason. The market cannot be cleared.

Now consider the special case of bureaucracy. There is no market or cash price for bureaucratic services. How, then, can the supply of bureaucracy be balanced with the demand? It can't be. The "market" cannot be cleared. The output of bureaucracy is thus doomed to perpetual glut or shortage, with the same frightful waste of economic and human resources. With no market data available, we can only guess at the real supply and demand picture under bureaucracy. My guess is that the demand for government favors (i.e., privileges or other people's tax dollars) is not and never will be satisfied. On the other hand, I have little doubt that the supply of bureaucrats, regulators, government inspectors, and all, is vastly greater than the market can swallow. Whatever the imbalances, they cannot be corrected. Unless we put a stop to it, the bureaucracy will go on wasting lives and resources until there is nothing left in the country to steal.

VII

WHY BUREAUCRACY GROWS

Granted that work (and especially paperwork) is elastic in its demands on time, it is manifest that there need be little or no relationship between the work to be done and the size of the staff to which it may be assigned . . . . Politicians and taxpayers have assumed (with occasional phases of doubt) that a rising total in the number of civil servants must reflect a growing volume of work to be done. Cynics, in questioning this belief, have imagined that the multiplication of officials must have left some of them idle or all of them able to work for shorter hours. But this is a matter in which faith and doubt seem equally misplaced. The fact is that the number of officials and the quantity of work are not related to each other at all.

— C. Northcote Parkinson

The U.S. Office of Education was a tiny, fact-finding body in 1939 when it was incorporated into a new, larger bureau called the Federal Security Agency. Few remember what the FSA was, but everyone is thoroughly familiar with what it became. After fourteen years, the FSA was promoted to the cabinet and changed its title to the U.S. Department of Health, Education, and Welfare. It began life with a budget of about $4 billion. After another twenty-six years, its budget now approaching $200 billion a year, HEW was seen to be great with child. And like some colossal whale calving, it was delivered of

143

a whole new Department of Education. In forty years of gestation, the tiny education bureau had grown into a cabinet department with *152 offices* of its own and a budget of $12 billion. For starters. Its compound growth rate for the period must have outstripped a Ponzi game.

This is a choice but by no means unusual example of a phenomenon we must explain. Why does bureaucracy inevitably grow and grow and grow? We have looked at endless examples of its handiwork, and find them to be frustrating, wasteful, rigid, harmful, ominous, and insane. We certainly cannot explain bureaucratic growth by its great and good works. We have peered deeply into its origins, but this does not explain the growth factor either; we have not seen any rousing public welcome for nomad warriors. We have looked into its political nature. Can we explain bureaucratic growth by this country's great love for politicians? Not exactly. What force is it then that can convert one little bureau into 152 clones and cabinet status? Something must account for bureaucratic growth, for grow it does, despite its being universally detested; despite all the harm and waste it causes.

Professor Parkinson offers an amusing insight about why we put up with an expanding bureaucracy. We are simply assuming that all those bureaucrats are there to do something. This, he points out, is a terrible mistake. When we see a whole legion of bureaucrats, we assume they are doing something very important — an even greater blunder. There is no basis at all for such assumptions. Bureaus, as we have seen, do not operate in the world of *doing things* with concrete purpose and clear goals. Their only purpose is to be what the reigning politicians say they should be, and move as far as they can up toward the fat end of the public trough. Certainly they are not there to "do something important" as the rest of us would understand the term. Nor does the *number* of bureaucrats, however great, mean anything, as Professor Parkinson observes. The work in a bureau has no relation whatsoever to the number of people who do it. For all anyone knows, millions of bureaucrats are employed to send each other memos. From all the reports I get, this seems to be exactly the case. Since any number can be employed in useless paper shuffling, it is clear enough that Parkinson is right, and that there is no relation between warm bodies and *work*. We eliminate workload as a factor in bureaucratic growth.

Yet here we have two solid hints at factors that do indeed promote bureaucratic growth despite its cost to society. The first is simply greed — that impulse to move up to the fat end of the trough. To get a fat salary for doing nothing. To live off the people. This impulse, combined with the license to steal that is the State, has catastrophic implications for humankind.

The second hint has to do with the way bureaucrats attain power and position. Bureau chiefs are paid, and their agencies are funded, according to how many warm bodies they command. It is obviously in their interest, therefore, to round up all the warm bodies possible, never mind if the personnel do anything. To do this, the administrator need only persuade Congress that he is doing great things; and his success in acquiring warm bodies is already evidence of this. Everything else, the increase in pay and prestige, is built into the law.

There are other and I think equally valid ways of looking at the factors of bureaucratic growth. Any of them is sufficient to explain the growth, but all offer different insights. Best, then, to consider the several growth theories systematically, one after another.

As we've seen, the first, and saddest, theory reduces to human greed, or more precisely, greed armed with a gun. We will return to this for serious discussion, for it is profound and far-ranging.

The second explanation is that growth is mandated by law. Ponder the proposition that the rank of a military commander is determined by the size of his command. Command of a company goes to a relatively inexperienced captain; of a regiment, to a more seasoned colonel; of a brigade, a brigadier general, who has even more experience. All this is perfectly sensible and logical. Yet there is a kicker in it, which is: all the pay and prestige of the position are based on the rank, and so derive from the *number* of people in the command. This poses no problem worth mentioning in the armed services; a commander cannot increase the size of his unit at will. But it is disastrous in civilian bureaus, which have the same arrangements for pay and promotion. In a civilian bureau, you *can* increase the number of employees with some ease, and this, as we've seen, has no bearing on the bureau's *work*. The temptation to add to one's own position as an administrator by hiring more people is ever present and naked. This all but guarantees all manner of finagling to increase bureaucratic personnel and size. So what if taxpayers get soaked in the process?

A third, and closely related, explanation is the *self-interest of the State*. This accounts for the fact that the State and society are not congruent, but rather are enemies, an us-or-them proposition — certainly true of the Old World State, if not the limited constitutional government devised in America. It follows that the State will always protect and enhance its own interests, at the expense of the interests of society. The State's own internal mechanisms are designed to serve its interests, including that of awarding rank by size of command, as just discussed. More important, its interest and its power depend on extending its reach and controls over society as far as possible. It therefore does everything it can to expand bureaucracy and its rules, a relatively easy matter, since it is in the driver's seat. All this expands its power and serves its interests.

Every State in history has behaved just this way, and there is no doubt that this explanation carries immense weight. And the State reasoning is impeccable, save for one fatal flaw: it forgets that it is parasitic, and that if it sucks the blood out of society, it too will die. Apparently the State's pride and glory blind it, for this inevitably is its end.

A fourth explanation might be called the drug addiction theory of bureaucracy. It can be stated as follows. Every bureaucratic intervention ("fix") where it does not belong causes economic damage and dislocation. This will create a need, or at least provoke an outcry, for new interventions to correct the damage. Another "fix." The bureaucracy intervenes again, ineluctably doing more damage, provoking yet further outcry, and so on. In this process, society becomes progressively more dependent on the bureaucratic drug, even as the drug ravages the social body. Again, there is a great deal to this. Such writers as Nock and Rose Wilder Lane have explored this phenomenon down to its deepest roots in natural law and human psychology, so there is no point in my repeating their findings.[1] One really need only recognize the counterproductive, anti-economic nature of bureaucratic measures to see how —and that — it works.

Rose Lane, who later became one of the great defenders of American liberty, was in early life a theoretical communist who observed firsthand the functioning of the young Soviet Union and other socialist experiments. From this experience she derived a view of bureaucratic growth that is similar to, but

---

[1] Nock, *op cit,* Rose Wilder Lane, *The Discovery of Freedom* (New York: The John Day Company, 1943).

broader than, the drug addiction theory. We might call it the social resistance theory.

What Mrs. Lane observed is that a bureaucratic intervention not only causes damage, it provokes resistance. The State must then *add to its police power* and intervene again, to quell resistance. And she was exactly right. Her observations explain what the "drug addiction" theory alone cannot, namely, that the intervention process is one of growing police power and totalitarianism, with military dictatorship the end product. History bears her out to the letter.

* * *

Lastly, I have my own modest theory of why federal agencies swell up like toadstools on a rotting log. This theory rests on two fundamental principles I will call Roche's first and second laws of bureaucratic growth. Namely: (1) The supply of human misery will rise to meet demand.

This simply extends the law of supply and demand[2], which everybody knows to be true, into a new and unexpected area: the bureaucratic "marketplace." I reason that bureaucratic spending to "solve" any given social problem in truth represents dollar demand for more of just that problem. If we create a market for misery by paying good money for it, the supply of misery will rise to meet demand. You want the halt, the lame, the blind? We got 'em. You want abject poverty?

---

[2] I take a small liberty here, but it does not change my findings one bit. Just as there is no such thing as a "germ" in microbiology and no "law of averages" in mathematics, there is no "law of supply and demand" in formal economics. There are laws of supply and laws of demand, but no one overriding law that covers both. Nevertheless, the term is both valid and very well understood. Economists themselves use it, as do professional financial writers; and so shall I.

We got that on special this week.

Any honest social worker will confirm this phenomenon, from experience in the field. If Congress adjusts the qualifications for welfare — free money — potential recipients will adjust their lives to qualify. If Congress offers money to the disabled, the number of handicapped people rises, and amazingly, they can prove their disabilities. If Congress offers money to the idle, as with unemployment relief, workers will stay idle as long as it pays them to. If Congress gives money to the sick, it creates an epidemic. All this is immutable in the economic law of supply and demand. In short, when Congress, and through it the bureaus, *demand* misery — in precisely the economic sense of offering dollars for it — misery is what they get every time. A generous public does not understand this, but I doubt that the point is lost on bureaucracy itself.

Roche's second law of bureaucratic growth is a refinement of the drug addict theory of bureaucracy, and goes like this: (2) The size of the bureaucracy increases in direct proportion to the additional misery it creates. Bureaucracy, in a word, increases geometrically while resources multiply only arithmetically. Thomas Malthus introduced this idea two centuries ago to argue that human reproduction must outrun our food supply, resulting in ultimate starvation. Malthus was thus the author of all our worries about overpopulation, but to date at least, it would seem that he got things backwards. Reproduction seems to be a factor of production, that is, food supply, and not the other way around. And it is productivity that has increased geometrically while reproduction has increased arithmetically. There has in fact been an immense growth of population since Malthus's time, with the result that something like one-ninth of all the people that have ever lived are alive now. The best and most recent scholarship also indicates that we have more resources than ever before. This will be no surprise to those who know how we develop resources.

Nevertheless, the same theory applied to bureaucracy, and in particular the parasitic form, is not only true but horrifying. Simply stated, State agencies can consume faster than we can produce. Never in sixty centuries of State history can I find a single exception to this. Over and over we see the same cycle: a civilization that rises in relative freedom and growing productivity, and falls in State excesses and consumption. Over and over we see the productive mechanisms destroyed by parasitism; anything worth stealing, stolen. The bureaucratic system, misapplied, cannot support human life.

In other words, in the State system, bureaucracy multiplies geometrically while the resources needed to support it, from the productive economy, grow only arithmetically. Political action creates an ever-increasing demand for bureaucratic intervention, which causes damage faster than society can repair it. Never knowing when to stop, the bureaucratic power continues to expand its interventions until society itself collapses.

The rise and fall of civilization is not everyone's cup of tea, so let's put it in contemporary terms. According to the conventional wisdom, we "collectively" identify some pressing social problem. This is certain to evoke cries for federal aid. Every interest group in the country is trained from birth to plead for federal funds, i.e., raid the treasury. Most, if not all, exist for no other purpose. All such pleas are at once amplified and echoed by like-minded interest groups, by academics, by reporters, by liberals or others who advocate government expansion, and most of all by the bureaucrats themselves, who stand to profit directly from an increase in their power. This chorus of interest groups therefore speaks for the new intervention in a loud and concentrated voice. It will recite all sorts of reasons why we all should support this new intervention; they will say it is compassionate and just and generous and oh-so right.

But opposition to the measure is faint and diffused among two hundred million people. The opponents are not organized. There are no "interest groups" to *oppose* the measure. And anything anyone says against the measure will be made to sound heartless and pro-misery — what? ! Are you in favor of cheating the poor and the helpless? Most of us are too generous and anti-misery to speak up at all. Few realize that the dispute is not about whether we should aid the needy (which we can do better through private charity), but rather, whether *this is an appropriate and just expansion of government power and taxation.* By bringing up the false issue of compassion, the coalition of special interests has already won the debate.

Professional politicians, who know exactly what is going on, now "report" to the people that the people are overwhelmingly in favor of the intervention. Congress then passes legislation that will supposedly deal with the problem. A new bureau is set up and funded, and taxes are increased accordingly. People, if they think about it at all, are extremely prone to make two false assumptions at this point. First, they assume that the legislation is democratic and representative because "everybody" is for it. In fact, only the few who stand to profit from it were for it, and they engineered a swindle. Second, we may assume that the problem has now been "taken care of." How anybody could believe this, given the un-broken record of bureaucratic disasters, I cannot imagine; but many do. It is faith almost child-like. The truth is, the problems have just begun. The intervention will create new problems and new demands for federal aid. It is this process that even now is taking us down the well-traveled road to absolutism and disaster.

We never seem to penetrate this swindle. It happens

over and over. It should be fundamental to our understanding: The bureaucracy cannot solve problems. It hasn't the tools to do so. It *creates* problems, and that is very much in its own interests. If bureaucrats actually solved the problems they are charged to, they would put themselves out of work, which is the gravest possible violation of the Bureaucratic Code. Bureaucrats never try to solve problems. Their business is to fund problems, or, occasionally, to license them for a fee.

In the process, we, the people, are ever so carefully coached and trained to ship every imaginable problem to the agency least equipped to deal with it — to the government. This has not always been so. In fact, the domestication of the free American — or if you prefer, the socialization — has only been achieved in the last few decades. Before that we were a fiercely independent bunch, too proud for the dole, and strong in our freedom. Now we are weak, eager for the tax-dollar benefits we think are a "right" even if somebody else earns them; and, hooked, we send more problems to Washington, D.C., where they cannot be solved.

The fact is, the government is in business to look after the government, and all the bureaus and agencies and offices it creates have but the one purpose of extending government power. Or if you want to put it crudely, they are there to buy votes, until the time that government domination is complete and votes are no longer needed. Consider this well, because in terms of governmental growth we are far along in the well-traveled road to decadence and annihilation. Not even America, for all its strength, can survive the ancient cycle. Either you and I get unhooked from our dependence on bureaucracy, or the soil of the earth will cover our proudest achievements, as it has in so many civilizations before ours.

To bring the point home, I am going to make you a bureau chief. I am going to present you with your own federal agency. You are a responsible person, so I know you will be determined to hold the line on spending, and to solve the social problem you've been assigned, even if it costs you your job. Yet, as if by primal instinct, your own bureau will create more of the difficulty it is supposed to deal with, and grow into a monster. And you can't stop it. And if you can't, what can we expect from a bureau chief whose only instincts are to follow the rules and enhance bureaucratic power, and never mind the problem?

This exercise, as I noted, is in the lighter vein, and you won't find a single measurable fact to support it — except that bureaucracy *does* grow, with disastrous consequences. But I am not straying from the truth. Roche's laws have been repeatedly confirmed by the (very) few people who have been through the bureaucratic mill and survived to tell the story. Life in the bureaucracy is terribly infectious, and not many come through unchanged. But if you know one who did, just ask.

* * *

Misery is discovered among the people! We go through the usual interest-group process, and Congress takes the usual legislative step, voting to create a new anti-misery agency. Let's put the initial funding, conservatively, at one billion dollars a year. That's not even one percent of the budget, not even close to it, a mere nothing — if, like Congress, you have no compunctions about spending the lifetime earnings of three or four thousand other people — three or four thousand productive *lives* — on this little project. After all, the government spends the earnings of around 60 million workers a year, and the *lifetime* earnings of two or three million — what's a few thousand more? What do

Congressmen know about earning a living, or anyway, how can they weigh the cost of spending thousands or millions of productive lives? You get your billion.

You are nominated as bureau chief and confirmed by the Senate. Your bureau will be called, appropriately, the Bureau to Abolish Misery (BAM), so that nobody will mistake your good purposes. You take the oath of office, swearing to uphold the Constitution, so help you God. Does it matter that you are sworn to abolish misery? Probably not. Does it matter that abolishing misery is not among the specified powers of the Constitution, and thus must be considered unconstitutional? That's between you and God. But you're in the bureaucratic business now, so what matters a little oath to God? You are working for the government.

Your first step, of course, is to hire a staff. You will need assistant administrators, a comptroller, a large legal department — all bureaus have a large legal department, a technical department with statisticians, mathematicians, computer specialists and so on, policy advisors, a property officer, clerk-typists to do the work, and, naturally, professional misery fighters. You will also need office space for all these people, needless to say, and for many more, the need for whose services will soon be apparent.

Of course you can't hire just anybody for these positions; you need highly qualified people. You will have to offer salaries — and this is required by law anyway —that are "competitive" with, which means higher than, those for "comparable" jobs in private business, of which there are none. So you offer attractive salaries for the right people. You also offer some fringe benefits that business cannot match, not least the *federal exemption from Social Security and its payroll taxes.* (The feds are no fools. They know what kind of a deal you get from Social Security. That's why they exempted themselves from it and set up their own, much more generous, pension plan.) Naturally you get the staff you want, but it does cost a bit.

Next you'll need some reasonably comfortable offices in a suitable location, which are not easy to find in Washington, D.C. You also want ample parking space, which is impossible to find in the District. Congress and the senior bureaucrats have already staked out all the parking. In any case, you end up spending a little bit more of your budget than you intended, getting set up. No matter, now you are in business, and you still have the usual 10% of your budget left to do what you set out to do — fight misery. That's still $100 million — not exactly small change in this world.

Unfortunately, nobody notices that BAM exists. You don't have any miserable clients. You will have to make a splash and let them know you are in business. So you hire a crack publicity staff, putting another dent in your dwindling budget. You have them work up a glowing report about BAM getting set up, headlined "New Agency Expeditiously Abolishes Misery." You send copies to Congress, other agencies, and the media, in that order.

In the ensuing publicity, a great many would-be miserable people learn about BAM. The law of supply and demand takes over. The law says: if you increase the dollar demand for a given commodity, the supply will rise to meet demand. What have you done by announcing your billion-dollar budget for abolishing misery? You have increased the dollar demand for misery by exactly one billion dollars. The market supply of misery must rise to meet this demand. This never fails. Soon there are long lines of wretched people in your offices, hat in hand. You hire more misery fighters to accommodate them.

BAM grows.

But you're already in trouble. After spending most of your budget to get set up, you don't have nearly enough money left to abolish misery. Indeed, your funds are being exhausted at an alarming rate. There is too much misery chasing too few dollars. You order your staff to check applicants' misery qualifications rigorously. Many clients get shortchanged or left out in the cold, and this makes them more miserable than ever. Some of them write spirited letters to their Congressmen, pointing out how miserable they are and making all manner of unpleasant remarks about heartless government. In the meantime, you send an urgent request to Congress for an emergency appropriation. Congress, which has other things on its mind, such as how to spot FBI men in mufti, and which is all in favor of abolishing misery anyway, gets the message. It votes to double your budget.

BAM grows. Taxes nudge higher.

You are back in business. The new funds ease the problem temporarily, but the law of supply and demand continues to function flawlessly. More people find out about BAM from the media and apply for relief. The friends and relatives of your BAM clients also prove to be very miserable, and they come around too. Soon the lines in your offices are longer than ever. You hire more misery clerks and send a report to Congress and the press on what a fine job BAM is doing abolishing misery.

BAM grows.

The lines of miserable people keep getting longer. They almost seem to be coming out of the woodwork. Their very lives are changed by the misery payments. It's not enough money, they complain to reporters. Their misery payment is barely enough to scrape by on, and that makes them miserable. This gets widely reported. You have your staff send out stiff letters to the press, pointing out that you are doing the best job you can to abolish misery on a very tight budget. The stories continue. In the publicity, more miserable people find out about BAM and seek relief.

You will have to go back to Congress for more money. This time you are asked to testify before a House subcommittee, to explain the situation. You have your growing PR staff prepare the presentation. The congressmen are not unsympathetic. You explain that America is far more miserable than Congress had originally thought. You riffle through your flip chart, showing the facts and figures. The subcommittee reports favorably on your request.

Congress sizes this up carefully. It's pretty plain that abolishing misery is politically popular. Mail has been heavy on that point. Constituents are begging to have their misery relieved. And the booming business at the Bureau to Abolish Misery wraps up the point. On the other hand, the pro-misery people are obviously weak and disorganized. No pro-misery lobby exists, few unfriendly editorials have appeared, and hostile mail is just the usual grousing from taxpayers who have to pay the bills. Congress votes a supplemental increase to BAM's emergency appropriation, thoughtfully sending out notices on this vote to the press and to concerned constituents.

BAM grows. Taxes increase perceptibly.

Now so many wretched people are lining up in your offices that your staff falls farther and farther behind in the paperwork. Services get slower and slower. You hire more clerks and open new windows, but the jam-up keeps getting worse. A few conservative newspapers run editorials highly critical of the waste and inefficiency in BAM. One says it should be abolished. Several senators get on your case.

You hire some really top-notch PR people to rally support for BAM on the hill. Experience has taught you that to get ahead in your mission, you have to have clout. Clout means making a favorable impression in the right places, i.e., where the money is, i.e., in Congress. Your PR team works up a great presentation. You send them out to lobby in all the right places, carefully timing it to sway congressional consideration of your regular annual appropriation. Your PR people are persuasive in arguing that BAM is abolishing misery as best it can on its puny $2.5 billion budget. They say misery is so pervasive, and BAM is doing such an important job, that your budget should be quadrupled. Congress ponders this, cuts your budget request with considerable fanfare, "to fight inflation," and allows you triple your previous appropriation, including supplemental emergency funding, which is exactly what you wanted. You don't tell the press that you and two key senators worked out just this appropriations strategy over a fancy dinner in Georgetown.

BAM mushrooms. Taxes increase again.

Your competition in the private sector slowly withers. Private misery insurance becomes less and less profitable, and is finally dropped by all the big insurance companies. Donations to charities drop off sharply, so they have little money to relieve misery. You are approaching a monopoly in the misery relief field. All the people who used to turn to charity or buy misery insurance become BAM clients, and the lines of misery supplicants in your offices get longer and longer. This calls for another emergency supplemental appropriation, which the House passes quietly, in a voice vote, without dissent.

BAM grows. Taxes rise.

You outgrow your original offices, and rent a whole office building just outside the District for your headquarters staff. Moving the bureau will be a headache and will disrupt services to the miserable, but there's no way to avoid it. You also set up nine regional offices at key points around the country, and these in turn set up satellite offices in most sizeable cities. This makes it much easier for miserable people to apply for relief. The wretched respond handsomely, lining up at BAM offices from coast to coast.

BAM grows. Taxes rise.

By now your personnel roster has become the third largest of any federal agency. Almost all of your people find their jobs extremely pleasant, their salaries adequate, their surroundings comfortable, and best of all, their jobs secure. They have none of those nagging worries about their jobs they used to have working in private business. Here you have made tremendous headway in your mission: *misery is at least 95% abolished* on your BAM staff. They become happily settled in, that is to say entrenched, that is to say, lifers. They themselves would become terribly miserable if they ever succeeded in the mission and abolished misery — they would be out of a job! But that is not possible. Monthly misery payments do not make anybody less miserable. And if they did, they would be prohibited by law! The regulations make it *very clear* that recipients must lead genuinely grim, miserable lives to get the payments. And so they do. Enforcing this "means test" creates a monumental paperwork problem, but how else can BAM — and Congress — be sure you are not making misery payments to people who are not really miserable? But questions like these need never concern you so long as the law of supply and demand remains in force. The more dollar demand you create for misery, the more misery the market will supply, and it will be the genuine article. BAM and its mission are utterly safe, as far into the future as one can see.

BAM grows. Taxes rise.

You personally, as an eleven-digit federal officer

(going on twelve), become entitled to a chauffeur-driven government limousine. As a modest person you worry that it might look bad, but everybody says otherwise. They say it's important for you to use the limo, so that you become a *visible symbol* of how *crucial* the job of abolishing misery has become to this great nation. And they are right. You take the limo.

BAM is having a banner year. Taxes rise.

Not everything is coming up roses, however. Quite the contrary. Rumors circulate that misery fraud is rampant in your agency. The sensationalist press charges that BAM is going to be investigated for "corruption." A congressman from Iowa gets all over you and makes numerous speeches in and out of Congress calling for a complete housecleaning. In due course a congressional committee investigates. It finds that certain rotten apples in the BAM barrel have used their offices to take graft and kickbacks, and to put happy relatives on the misery rolls. Altogether there are 152 indictments, and several thousand other BAM employees sigh with relief when they are missed. It is a trying time, but your PR staff fights back with a promise to make a clean sweep, and by arguing that this sort of thing is inevitable because BAM is so pinched for funds in its great task. You ask for an emergency appropriation to hire auditors. With appropriate fanfare, you beef up your internal enforcement staff and launch your own investigation. You fire eleven people you never did like anyway, and announce that the problem has been solved.

BAM continues to grow despite its problems. Taxes rise.

As if one scandal weren't enough, an audit reveals that 27% of your misery payments have been going to unqualified, cheerful people. This is little worse than average for federal programs, but it causes some stir. You hire more auditors, with fanfare. Congress tightens up eligibility rules, but softens the blow by increasing your appropriation. Your paperwork problems multiply, so you have to hire more people to handle it, including three of the eleven people you fired.

BAM grows. Taxes rise.

The law of supply and demand continues to function perfectly. Every time your appropriation increases, more miserable people apply for relief. The more clients you have, the higher the appropriations you have to seek from Congress every year. But Congress will comply when you demonstrate how many miserable people need help. And the following year even more miserable people will want relief.

BAM grows much larger. Tax rates are "adjusted."

In a brainstorming session your PR people come up with a really sharp idea: Misery Stamps. You like it, and have them work out the details for a presentation. In a few months you appear before a congressional committee with your flip charts to make the case for Misery Stamps. Not only will Misery Stamps help abolish misery, you argue, it will cut down on paperwork in BAM. Congress likes it, and soon BAM is issuing billions of dollars worth of Misery Stamps to the miserable. One can spend them just like money and all the stores accept them. In fact, they are money.

BAM grows. Inflation rages.

About this time a hot young staffer in the legislative office points out that BAM is too big for one bureau. You are fighting the greatest social problem of our times. Business is booming. It is time for the amoeba to split. What you should do, the young man suggests, is specialize: set up seven new offices, directly under yours (here he shows you a new organization chart he has thoughtfully drawn up, with the seven offices in place). The new offices would handle specific kinds of misery. You should have special offices for the halt, the lame, the blind, the elderly, the minority surnames, the resentfully nonupwardly-mobile, and afternoon soap opera junkies. You can't reach all this misery without these special offices, he argues. You like it, promote him on the spot, and reach for the phone to put it in motion.

BAM grows. Tax rates are "adjusted" another point.

Ideas dance. You brainstorm it with the same young man, now your personal assistant, and a few of your best PR people. You think of at least *fifty* groups of wretched people who aren't being reached now, but who could be reached through special BAM programs and offices. Your assistant points out that if you can feed a new office onstream every week or two, BAM should reach cabinet status in eighteen months at the outside. A serene, presidential-prospect smile crosses your face as you reach for the phone.

BAM swells. Taxes rise sharply.

The dream comes true, almost on schedule. BAM is awarded cabinet rank, and now becomes the U.S. Department to Abolish Misery — DAM! Along with the award comes a sharp increase in your appropriation, now well into twelve digits. You are confirmed as the first DAM secretary. Congratulations!

DAM mushrooms. Taxes mushroom. Inflation passes 30%.

With cabinet rank, DAM enjoys a startling change in the public and media attitude. People stand in awe. Reporters are extremely deferential. Publicity about DAM abounds. You personally are mentioned regularly in the news and gossip columns. You have arrived.

DAM continues to mushroom. Taxes rise. Inflation rages. The economy slips into a sharp recession, despite the blizzard of paper money and bank credit.

Now the Grand Effect takes over. Between DAM's twelve-digit budget and similar efforts by your bureaucratic colleagues, the tax burden *creates* severe poverty all over the country. More and more marginal taxpayers are pushed into the destitute bracket. Now *they* become miserable and apply for relief. As the recession deepens, millions are thrown out of work and become desperate. They too qualify for misery relief. The process feeds on itself. The millions of newly miserable people getting relief increases the tax burden and inflation so sharply that even more taxpayers are forced to take relief. The number of productive taxpayers dwindles rapidly, while the misery rolls swell enormously. Government printing presses work night and day printing more money, but the economy crumbles. Millions more become unemployed and apply for misery relief. You go on national TV and promise relief for all. Business at DAM has never been better.

DAM grows. The economy collapses. Tax rates increase, but nobody can pay the taxes. Misery payments are financed entirely by fiat money, but the payments don't buy anything.

At this point, practically everybody in the country is unutterably miserable, except, of course, the bureaucrats. The entire country is your client at DAM. Yours is the Cinderella story of world bureaucracy.

On this cheerful note, we take leave of our tale. It is time to go anyway; the Barbarians are at the gate.

* * *

My tale was playful. Its message is anything but. Every effort to eradicate "misery" through the taxing power of the central State is a contradiction in terms, and foredoomed.

The State has no resources to fight poverty or misery. It has no money to give the people that it has not first taken from the people. Much of what it takes, it keeps, to pay its own, enormous, bureaucratic expenses. It is a matter of mathematical certainty, therefore, that the people *always* get back far less than they contribute. Or put it this way: the process invariably leaves the people with *more* poverty and the government with *less*. This should persuade you, if nothing else has, that it is always in the State's interest to *make* you poor and miserable. It's the perfect way to keep their hands in your pockets.

* * *

Let us return now to the point I posed earlier, namely that in its deepest roots, the impulse toward bureaucratic growth is fueled by simple human greed. For this, we turn again to the insights of Albert Jay Nock in his classic 1935 essay, *Our Enemy, the State*. This work developed the earlier sociological research of Franz Oppenheimer, who had observed that throughout history, without exception, "Wherever opportunity offers, and man possesses the power, he prefers political to economic means for the preservation of his life." Baldly stated, men would rather steal than earn a living *if* they have a way to do so easily.

From Herbert Spencer and Henry George, Nock had learned "the formula that man tends always to satisfy his needs and desires with the least possible exertion."

These two basic principles of behavior come together in an almost blinding insight about the human condition. Nock recalled that it occurred at a luncheon with his friend Edward Epstean, to whom his book was dedicated. He described the incident in his autobiography:

> I do not recall what subject was under discussion at the moment; but whatever it was, it led to Mr. Epstean's shaking a forefinger at me, and saying with great emphasis, "I tell you, if self-preservation is the first law of human conduct, exploitation is the second."
>
> The remark instantly touched off a tremendous flashlight in

my mind. I saw the generalization which had been staring me in the face for years ... If this formula (of Spencer and George) were sound, as unquestionably it is, then certainly exploitation would be an inescapable corollary, because the easiest way to satisfy one's needs and desires is by exploitation ....

In an essay which I published some time ago (*Our Enemy, the State*), having occasion to refer to this formula, I gave it the name of Epstean's law .... *Man tends always to satisfy his needs and desires with the least possible exertion.*

(Original emphasis)

Armed with this insight, Nock demolished all pretense that the State could ever become a benevolent institution or serve the interests of society. The State *is the organization of the political means.* Its sole purpose is the economic exploitation of one class by another. The State originated historically for purposes of exploitation, and exploitative it remains; it cannot change its nature. So swift and telling were his arguments that the whole battle was over in five pages. Washed away were all the attractions of centralism, all the romantic Marxist notions that the State, once it became total, would coincide with the interests of society and "wither away."

Nock was careful to distinguish between "government," essentially a negative or non-intervening form of organization whose only interests are justice and defense, and the State of the Old World, which is ever an exploiter. The Founding Fathers made the same distinction and made every effort to limit our own government to its rightful purposes. But the distinctions were chipped away over the years, and finally destroyed in the legislative carnival called the New Deal. Ever since we have had, in essence, a State of the Old World type. Ever since its exploitations have grown year after year, its appetite increasing with every bite. I believe that this is the whole political problem of our time.

The only "if" in Epstean's law, the one observed by

Oppenheimer, is: "Whenever opportunity offers, and man possesses the power," he will turn to the political means: exploitation. Confiscation. Theft.

The underlying question is, what is the easiest way for us to satisfy our needs? In a state of pure or relative freedom, the economic means is clearly the easiest. Stealing is too much work and much too risky. If you arm yourself to steal, people will arm themselves to defend themselves and their property. If you organize a whole band of thieves, the defenders will organize a militia. And they will show you no kindness if you are caught, as inevitably you will be. Under "government" as Nock and the Founding Fathers conceived it, the economic means remains clearly superior. In other words, under freedom, Epstean's law dictates that men will earn their living instead of turning to theft; it is simply easier. Honesty becomes more fruitful than greed, and men prosper.

What changed the equation was successful conquest by the nomad marauders, and the genesis of the State. It is the State, and nothing else, that makes it easier to steal than earn. The State is a license to steal. Physical fear of the conqueror turns into psychological dependence; the State is accepted as the supreme power, a god, a protector and dispenser of justice. Its agents assume the aura of a priestly class, in the vestments of authority; and its exactions become irresistible. No longer can subjects question the right of the State to take what it will, for their minds are enslaved along with their bodies. The State is god. The honest dealings of men give way to greed, and greed to glory. The masses are forced not to bake bread but to build pyramids. Such is the nature of things.

With the introduction of a true State in America, the workings of Epstean's law dictated that men would go to Washington, D.C., for the ancient rituals. Men who do not respect the property of others. Men who have not the moral rigor to avoid the easy way. Uncivilized, greedy men: heirs of the ancient nomads. It is their greed that builds the American superstate and praises its glory.

Only now, fifty years after it began, do we see the first glimmer that other men, men of principle, men who do not choose the easy way, can go to Washington with popular support and try to restore the American concept. But so far it is only a glimmer, and terribly hard for those who act on our behalf. The best thing we can do for them, and for ourselves, is to understand. Our enemy is greedy, and his every appeal addresses the greed within ourselves. If we know this and resist, we give him no refuge; only then will his swindles fail.

VIII

WHOSE SIDE IS CONGRESS ON?

> . . . we see how ignorance and delusion concerning the nature of the State combine with extreme moral debility and myopic self-interest . . . to enable the steadily accelerated conversion of social power into State power . . . It is a curious anomaly. State power has an unbroken record of inability to do anything efficiently, economically, disinterestedly or honestly; yet when the slightest dissatisfaction arises over the exercise of social power, the aid of the agent least qualified to give aid is immediately called for . . . . "Ever since society has existed," says Herbert Spencer, "disappointment has been preaching, 'Put not your trust in legislation'; and yet the trust in legislation seems hardly diminished."
>
> One may put it in a word that . . . the State is by its nature concerned with the administration of law — law, which the State manufactures for the service of its own primary ends.
>
> — Albert Jay Nock

You and I know that bureaucracy is strangling the country. So does the Congress of the United States; at least, they hear about the problem every day. So why, we wonder, isn't Congress doing anything about it? But can we really be sure it isn't? I decided to check.

Certainly Congress has the power to stop bureaucratic abuses. It has the power to create bureaus, and can as easily abolish them. Equally important, it has power

over the national purse. It can limit bureaucratic interference to any degree desired by limiting spending.
Given these powers, it would seem pretty plain that
Congressmen, whatever they tell the folks back home,
are not doing much of a job of reining in the bureaucracy. Still, I wanted to be sure of this, so I went through
an entire year's legislative output to answer this question: what is Congress doing about bureaucracy?

The unequivocal answer is, *making things worse.* In the
year I looked at, Congress took not one step that I could
find to reduce the bureaucracy or its grasp. It took many
steps that *created* new bureaus or enlarged bureaucratic
power. This precisely supports the lessons of history
that I mentioned earlier, that sovereigns *never* surrender
power voluntarily, but rather seize any excuse to expand
their power at the expense of their citizens (or their
neighbors).

The year I examined, for no particular reason, was
1976. That, of course, was the Bicentennial year, so if
anything, it should have been a bit more productive than
usual in measures that reflected the American heritage
and regard for liberty. In fact, it produced no such
measures at all. So much for our traditions and dreams.

I looked at every piece of legislation that was signed
into Public Law in 1976. The experience was unnerving,
proving once again that if you like law or sausage, you
should never watch it being made.

There were 383 bills enacted into law over the period
(January 28 to October 22, 1976). That's a little over one
a day, on average for the year. Costs were not stated, but
averaged around $1.5 *billion* per law — no small feat, as
we shall see. Let me remind you that it took the
government fifteen presidential administrations and
seventy years to spend its first billion dollars. In 1976, it
took only sixteen hours to do it, and today, it's down to
about eleven hours.

I classed the 383 laws into what seemed useful categories. These were subjective and some overlap resulted, but the results were good enough. I have rounded the final figures a bit for convenience.

Of the 383, I found only 19 that *looked* like laws — 5%. These were the Thus-and-So Acts. Another 20 or so "provided" or "required" this or that, usually something trivial. Five more "prohibited" something, again usually trivial. Taking all these together, we have something less than 12% — one-eighth of the Congressional effort — devoted to serious and not-so-serious lawmaking.

What do you suppose was the most popular Congressional activity, if not passing laws? Exactly. Spending money. Of course. There were 20 appropriations bills, most undoubtedly massive. In addition, more than 70 bills "authorized funds for" things, some of these also massive, some not. Yet another 15 authorized *emergency* or supplemental funds on top of the regular funds. (I think I saw one for the Bureau to Abolish Misery, but I can't be sure.) Over 27% of the legislation was for spending. Your money, of course.

You may not guess the next most popular theme, so I'll tell you. It was amending past legislation, which is to say, correcting old mistakes. Which is to say, making new mistakes in place of the old ones. Over 75 bills were for this purpose — the biggest single category on my list, and a pretty good indication of how good Congress is at legislating in the first place. Another 15 "extended" some law, agency, or mistake, so I'll add these in as amendments of sorts. In some cases, they were clearly procrastination — renewing the mistakes with an eye to "amending" them later. All told we have about 90 laws in this category, an error rate of about 25%. Any company that handled its business that sloppily would be bankrupt tomorrow.

Over 50 bills were devoted to miscellaneous

"authorizings," mostly trivial, some downright weird. Nearly 30 others were hopelessly miscellaneous, and as a rule, even weirder.

My favorite category, and clearly the same to many legislators, was laws naming buildings after prominent politicians. There were more than 20 of them, and several more that named things like parks and rivers, not necessarily after politicians.

Fifteen or so did some quiet slushing, increasing benefits for this favored group or that. (Of course most of the slush was in the main appropriations bills.) Some 20 "established" things like parks or wilderness areas, in all cases by intruding into previously private domain. Five established new federal agencies outright (but other legislation increased the total considerably).

Finally, two increased the federal debt limit. Have you ever heard of a law that decreased the federal debt limit?

You can't really get the flavor of this without some specifics, so let's have a closer look. The first Public Law of the bunch was normal enough — a gigantic appropriation for the departments of HEW and Labor. But the second order of business was "providing for starling and blackbird control in Kentucky and Tennessee." No doubt an important matter. The third "Relat(ed) to the presentation by the United States to Israel of a statue of Abraham Lincoln to be donated by Leon and Ruth Gildesgame of Mount Kisco, N.Y." Awfully nice of the Gildesgames, but why on earth do we need an act of Congress for this? Is this what we pay 435 congressmen and 100 senators, plus their staffs, to do? (Answer: yes.)

The next bill was "to amend the National Portrait Gallery Act to redefine the term 'portraiture.'" Now I ask you, during the last campaign, did your congressman happen to mention anything about redefining portraiture? No. Did you even know there was a National Portrait Gallery, much less an Act? No. Is this how you want your representatives spending your money (as opposed to your private contributions)? No. Is this what legislators should be spending their exceedingly expensive time on? No. Are U.S. senators and representatives qualified to define English words? Ridiculous. What do you think of this? Please go outside to express your opinion; children may be listening.

So what's going on here? We're already four laws into the season, and only the first has any substance — and the substance of that is to appropriate, that is, confiscate, unbelievable sums for unbelievable purposes. The others had to do with shooting birds, a statue, and redefining the word "portraiture." Strange indeed. Naturally it gets worse.

On February 5, the Rail Services Act becomes law. This is one of the ones I put down as "real" law. Guess what becomes law on February 6? A bill "making certain technical corrections in Public Law 94-210, the Rail Services Act." Here is indisputable proof they got things screwed up the first time, without even waiting for the disastrous consequences in private life.

Other big doings in February:

— "Proposing establishment of programs for the benefit of producers and consumers of rice." Slush, needless to say. Or to put matters just a bit more plainly, the government is announcing that it is going to take away from you the money you earn, to give to rice growers, because they are very, very nice folks. What benefit this can have for "consumers" of rice is impossible to imagine. Let us be grateful they aren't trying to feed Asia with laws like this.

— "Authorizing the Secretary of Transportation to release restrictions on the use for airport purposes of certain property conveyed to the city of Elkhart, Kansas." Good for Elkhart, and remember, these laws cost on average a billion and a half dollars apiece.

— . . . acquisition of Wetlands . . . authorizing additional funds for . . . Extending until September 12, 1976, the current prohibition against . . . amending the effective date of . . . making a certain film available for . . .

A billion here, a billion there; pretty soon you're talking about real money. March roars in like a lion:

— "Relating to the detail, pay, and succession to duties of the Assistant Commandant of the Marine Corps." You've heard of the six-million-dollar man; how about a billion-and-a-half-dollar assistant?

— "Making supplemental appropriations . . . for the Library of Congress James Madison Memorial Building," which by some fluke got "additional funds" in February. It's so hard to make ends meet these days.

— "Authorizing the Secretary of the Interior to construct and operate the Polecat Beach area of the Shoshone extension unit, Pick-Sloan Missouri basin program, Wyoming." Whether the beach is really for polecats is not revealed. Nor is the identity of Pick and Sloan, but you can lay long odds that they were either politicians or politically influential.

So far, the mental prowess required for legislating would not seem to be very high, agreed? For which we may be profoundly grateful. But suppose even a minor matter comes along that requires some degree of expertise — are we in good hands?

— "Authorizing the sale and shipment of carbonyl chloride by the Department of Defense."

What's this? What is carbonyl chloride? Do you know? I don't. Does your congressman know? I'll bet not. Why is the Defense Department shipping and selling the stuff? Is it safe? Is it wise? What is DoD doing in the sales business anyway?

The next day, a casual entry:

— "Making a supplemental appropriation in the

amount of $2.143 billion for purposes of upgrading the Nation's railroad facilities through fiscal year 1977."

Precisely $2.143 billion, huh? If everything is so neatly figured out to the last paltry million, why is this a supplemental appropriation? Why this sum extra, now? If all 100 senators and 435 representatives spent the whole day poring over this request, each and every one of them would still be responsible for over $4 million worth of spending. Can *you* deal responsibly with $4 million in costs in one day? And if you can, are you confident that your 534 colleagues will do just as well? But this is absurd: neither you nor they know how to run a railroad, much less decide how to decide that every last penny has been spent to best advantage. There may be somebody in Congress who worked for a railroad once, but most members couldn't carry their own bags aboard without help. They are politicians, not railroad managers. They make monumental decisions like this cheerfully and without a second thought because they cannot grasp that there is anything important about it.

Congressmen haven't the foggiest idea what the money means. The human mind, and certainly the government mind, does not easily grasp such large numbers. What's $2.143 billion to a congressman? Small change. A minor fraction of one percent of the budget. But those dollars represent the toil and struggle and efforts and dreams of real people. In this case, the figure consumes the entire working *lives* of three or four thousand people. Congress cannot conceivably understand the thousands of years of effort by these folks, their dreams, their hopes, that it wipes away with the most casual vote. A few billion extra for socialized rail service — what's that. Somebody will take care of it. Put the cost on everybody, and it's a crummy $50 or so a family — what's that. Nothing. Maybe *you* think you should spend $50 carefully, but Congress could care less. This is just a fraction of a percent of what it spends. Esteemed colleagues, let us vote "yea" and get on to more important matters. It's only money. We still have 99+% of the budget to spend.

— "To revise the per diem allowance for members of the American Battle Monuments Commission." You probably didn't realize that battle monuments had or needed a commission, much less one with revised per diems; revised upwards, no doubt.

— "To provide full exploration and development of the Naval petroleum reserves and to permit limited production from NPRs No. 1, 2 and 3." If I'm not mistaken, this means getting some oil out of the famed Teapot Dome, fifty years after the scandal. A good idea, perhaps. More likely it is a panicky federal response to the "energy crisis" it created by putting price controls on the oil industry.

— "Adding a new chapter to the Bankruptcy Act to provide for the adjustment of debts of major municipalities." Uh oh. Who are they bailing out here — New York, Cleveland? Behind this new chapter in the bankruptcy law is something new in American history: the spectre of great cities going belly up due to their Byzantine tax codes, corruption, and gross financial mismanagement. And who's going to rescue them? The whizzes in Washington who manage our national finances so well. As if our congressmen could understand and correct the hopelessly snarled municipal finances that brought the problem on.

— "To convey approximately one acre of land to the Twenty-nine Palms Park and Recreation District, California." Which has just become some of history's most expensive real estate.

— "To designate April 13, 1976, as Thomas Jefferson Day." It's a good thing the author of the Declaration of Independence was not around to witness this one; he'd gag.

— "To provide for the division of assets between the Twenty-nine Palms and the Cabazon band of Mission Indians." Now here, you'll agree, is a situation that every congressman will be fully conversant with — a money dispute among Indian "bands." Well do I recall the congressional candidates speaking to just this issue last November. But even I didn't suppose that they would devote themselves to those 29 palms twice in one week.

— "To authorize the erection in the District of Columbia of a statue of Bernardo De Galvez." Bernie, whoever you are, there went another congressional day and another billion and a half.

These mighty labors, and many more of the sort, have now carried us into May of 1976. Nineteen hundred seventy-six was our celebrated 200th year of independence. May is the month of any year you have to work to, to pay off your federal tax burden and become independent. Of course, you still have to work all of May and then some to pay your state and local bureaucrats, but after that you get to keep your own money. This is indeed independence.

Lots more laws in May:

— "To protect the public health by assuring the safety and effectiveness of medical devices." Now, really. Are they actually just getting around to regulating medical devices in 1976? Of course not. You can hardly buy a tongue depressor without a prescription and a note from HEW. This is the sort of law that sounds good to the public, so they pass it once a year or so. A law like this can make it into the books hundreds of times without anybody noticing.

— "To provide for the definition and punishment of certain crimes in accordance with the Federal laws in force within the special maritime and territorial jurisdiction of the U.S. when said crimes are committed by an Indian in order to insure equal treatment for Indian and non-Indian offenders." Well! It would seem that those pesky injuns are still causing trouble for the feds, and violating maritime and territorial jurisdiction as they please. How shall we deal with them? Very gently. They are, after all, Indians, and we keep hearing about the congressional concern for "Indians." Keep this in mind, for we will hear more on the subject.

— "To establish a Commission on Security and Cooperation in Europe," as if this were (a) possible and (b) desirable.

After many appropriations, meaning taxes, we move into June, with ethnic matters still burning:

— "Calling for the Department of Labor to collect, analyze and publish unemployment data relating to Americans of Spanish origin or descent." Pure bureaucratese, in conception and wording, for a piece of ethnic snoopery. This one has to do with those pesky Mexicans, who would be pleased to tell you that they are not Spanish. In fact, most would be pleased to answer to plain old "American." But the bureaucracy has a problem here. It cannot shower favors on underprivileged minorities unless it can *find* the minority and prove that it is discriminated against. For this it must not only snoop into ethnic concerns but *create* ethnic distinctions. If this strikes you as the worst possible taste and a gross violation of human dignity, you have not reckoned how far liberal legislators will go to show their "compassion."

— "To amend retroactively Department of Agriculture regulations pertaining to the computation of price support payments under the National Wool Act of 1954." Not only slush, but slush retroactive to 1954. One supposes that sheep raisers and wool makers can file amended slush forms to collect their extra benefits for the previous 22 years. The Lord is my shepherd, but the shepherds here are getting theirs in Washington, D.C.

Remember those killer bees?

— "To prohibit the importation and to prevent the spread of African Brazilian honey bees in the United States." And *that* takes care of *that,* eh? In another vote, the Senate voted 100 to 0 — almost unheard of — to prohibit the importation of killer bee semen. There was one small problem. Nobody then or now has the faintest idea how to obtain killer bee semen, or what to do with it if you get some. Anyway, here's the law that saved our country from the killer bees, and never mind that the bees bred themselves out of existence a thousand miles short of our borders.

There is another side to the story one rarely hears. The bees were deliberately bred for aggressiveness, and it worked. And they did kill some careless beekeepers in Brazil, perhaps as many as fifty over several years. (People die of bee stings in this country every year.) This gave the bees their bad reputation and the name "killer," at least in press and government circles that don't have anything to do with beekeeping. The Brazilian government set out to exterminate them. But the bees in fact were a great success; their aggressiveness made them enormous producers. It was the beekeepers who protested the government extermination. All the government managed to do was destroy the beekeepers' livelihood, while plenty of the bees were wild and loose. For years afterwards we had reports of them moving north a few hundred miles a year, losing their aggressiveness all the while. And then, finally, just about when all threat had vanished, the United States Senate voted unanimously to keep them out of the country. Perhaps our vigilant customs people could have fought them off at the border.

Back to the business at hand, which happens to be many more authorizings and tax grabs. These are done quietly; it is after all the bicentennial year. Let us move along toward July 4 and independence.

— "To extend for 30 days the Federal Energy Admin-istration." A big mistake. A dreadful mistake. The FEA not only escaped alive, but was awarded cabinet rank and the power to make the energy crisis perpetual. But just imagine, here was a time when this multi-squillion-dollar bureau was living on 30 days' authority.

— "Increasing to $700 billion through September 30, 1977, the temporary limit on public debt." *Temporary*, indeed! One wonders what good a "limit" is if it never limits anything.

This one says just about everything there is to say about congressional activity.

— "Expressing to Her Majesty, Queen Elizabeth II, United States appreciation for the bequest of James Smithson to the United States enabling the establish-ment of the Smithsonian Institution." There you have it, a Thank You note, and only a little more than a century and a half late.

We move into August. The next one is famous: "To establish and implement a national swine flu immuniza-tion program."

This is the best-known example of the government inventing a cure for which there is no known disease. Reports vary; some say there actually was a case of swine flu in Illinois, or maybe there was one in New Jersey. Others insist that there were no cases anywhere. Disease or no, the immunizing went forward with typical government dispatch, that is, near panic. Several people had an unusual reaction to the vaccine: they died on the spot. Others died within a day or two. Many more were paralyzed. To allay fears, President Ford got his shot publicly, with much fanfare, and lived through it. The government still faces more than a billion dollars worth of damage claims and lawsuits.

You may think I'm being unfair in these discussions by quoting just the silly stuff. Not so. There's plenty more where this comes from, and just as silly. Nevertheless, every so often something that looks like a real law comes along, and in the interests of even-handedness, I'll be happy to mention it. In fact, I've found an example: "To provide that meetings of Government agencies be open to the public." A wonderful idea. Exactly 200 years late, but welcome nonetheless.

— "To increase authorizations for activities of the Privacy Protection Study Commission." Now, what do you suppose a Privacy Protection Study Commission does? And why does it need those increased authorizations? Does it Study Privacy? In public? Does it Protect Commissions? In private? Will the Commission, after appropriate Study, recommend that the last law be repealed, so that government agencies can protect their privacy and *not* be open to the public?

Here's another sleeper: "To regulate mining activities within areas of the national park system."

Well, if you're going to do mining in parks, you ought to regulate it. If I'm not mistaken, this is a panic law, in the aftermath of the disclosure (mentioned earlier) that two different federal agencies had issued permits for mining in the Grand Canyon. Public comment at the time was somewhat uncomplimentary, so Congress did what it always does in these situations; it passed another law. How it managed not to prevent mining in the Grand Canyon in the first place, we'll never know.

Plenty of important business in October. There's always *so* much to do before Congress recesses.

— "To authorize the National Society of the Daughters of the American Revolution to acquire and dispose of property." One of the battle cries of the Revolution itself, in 1776, was "life, liberty and property." Why on earth do we need a law two centuries later "authorizing" a society of the Revolutionary War veterans' descendants to have property?

— "To suspend until July 1, 1978, duty on certain elbow prostheses if imported for charitable therapeutic use or for free distribution by certain public or private nonprofit institutions." Wonderful. But why was there a tariff on elbow prostheses in the first place? Do we tax wooden legs and glass eyes?

— "To amend the Alaska Native Claims Settlement Act so as to provide for the withdrawal of certain lands for the Village of Klukwan, Alaska." Glad *that's* taken care of.

— "To provide for the appointment of George Washington to the grade of General of the Armies of the United States." Yes, *that* George Washington. I'm sure he'd be pleased with this timely promotion, if he hadn't had the misfortune of passing away in 1799.

Remember all those laws about Indians? Get this: "Authorizing the President to proclaim the week of October 10 through 16, 1976, as 'Native American Awareness Week.' " Too late. Indians they are in Public Law, and Indians they will always be.

Between October 14 and 17, we have no fewer than ten bills naming buildings after politicians. (Recess is coming up soon.) The legislative season is fast running out, but let's look at one more piece of congressional efficiency:

— "Adding Alaska and Hawaii to the list of 48 states whose names are inscribed on the walls of the Lincoln National Monument."

Unseemly haste! And last:

— "To provide benefits for survivors of Federal Judges comparable to those received by survivors of Members of Congress."

There is good news indeed, providing that any of us can survive federal judges and members of Congress.

* * *

The lesson in this seems to me as sad as it is clear. There is no way this sort of congressional pother is ever going to bring bureaucracy under control. Congress just goes on adding to the problem all the time.

It seems to me further that representative government itself is failing us, and badly. In no way do these legislative efforts represent the real problems and needs of the American people. Our problems are a crushing tax burden, inflation (a tax), and a stagnant economy, all caused by just the sort of federal meddling that Congress continues to do.

If a solution is to be found, it must be soon and it must be drastic. We must take whatever steps are needed to rid ourselves of our dependence on the bureaucratic machine, and we must bring Congress back under control, and make it once again the representative body it was meant to be. If we are less than resolute, if we fail, then we will fall as all civilizations before us have, and the American light of freedom will flicker out.

Current political trends indicate that the problem of bureaucracy is uppermost in the minds of the American people, but it remains to be seen whether or not the problem can be effectively handled. It is easier to criticize than to make lasting correction. The future of the Republic may rest upon how effective that correction proves to be.

This book is not intended as a blueprint for that correction. Such correction must be fought out in the trenches of day-to-day definitions of public and private policy, separating legitimate and appropriate government action from the usurpations and abuses which must be eliminated. And *that* effort cannot be left solely in the hands of any political administration. The task is too great. To be successful, the effort must be supported by a high level of determination and understanding among all citizens. We must prefer the private sector, competition, self-determination and voluntary action; not only prefer but demand the chance to lead our lives in the same way earlier generations of Americans demanded the chance to lead theirs — as free men and women.

ABOUT THE AUTHOR

Dr. George Roche has served as President of Hillsdale College, Hillsdale, Michigan since 1971. He served for three and one-half years as President Reagan's appointed Chairman of the National Council on Educational Research. He is the author of five previous books, including *Legacy of Freedom*, *Frederic Bastiat: A Man Alone*, and *The Bewildered Society*, and hundreds of articles that have appeared in journals and magazines all over the world. In all these endeavors George Roche has consistently reflected a philosophy based on the Judeo-Christian heritage, individual liberty, free enterprise, and the values underlying the American Dream.